REG.
PRICE 12-83
STRAND PRICE
48¢
EACH

W9-BYC-592

Foreign State Enterprises

FOREIGN STATE ENTERPRISES

A Threat to
American Business

DOUGLAS F. LAMONT

Basic Books, Inc., Publishers

NEW YORK

Library of Congress Cataloging in Publication Data

Lamont, Douglas F
    Foreign state enterprises, a threat to American
business.

    Includes bibliographical references and index.
    1. Government business enterprises. 2. International
business enterprises. 3. Corporations, Foreign--United
States. I. Title.
HD3850.L33   338.8'8'0973   78-19818
ISBN 0-465-02482-3

Copyright © 1979 by Basic Books, Inc.
Printed in the United States of America
DESIGNED BY VINCENT TORRE
10 9 8 7 6 5 4 3 2 1

CONTENTS

Contents

PART FOUR
Nexus Strategies

PART FIVE
American Decisions

LIST OF TABLES

List of Tables

PREFACE

IN 1962, I bought a box of Charritos (Cheerios in Mexico) in a retail store called Conasupo. Why was I in a government-owned shop? For one thing, it sold packaged food items produced in Mexico more cheaply than the supermarkets. And for another, as a graduate student writing a doctoral dissertation, I had to live within my student stipend.

Six years later I returned to Mexico as an exchange professor.

This time I had the money to shop at Su Mesa and Gigante. I went to the Conasupo stores to ask questions. What class of people shopped here? What did they buy? What was stocked in the store? How large was the store? What was its volume?

To get to the Conasupo stores between Monterrey and Veracruz I had to buy gasoline from the only marketer south of the Rio Grande, Pemex (Petróleos Mexicanos, Mexican Petroleum Co.).

This became a habit. Between 1968 and 1973 I had gasoline pumped into my car by Brazil's Petrobrás (Petróleo Brasileiro, Brazilian Petroleum Co.), Argentina's YPF (Yacimientos Petroliferos Fiscales, Petroleum Fiscal Monopoly), France's CFP (Cie. Française des Pétroles, French Petroleum Company), and Italy's ENI (Ente Nazionale Idrocarburi, National Hydrocarbon Corporation). This service ranged from indifferent to good. Some did lube jobs.

Others could do motor work. A few even had restaurants where pasta was sold to hungry drivers on their way from Milan to Naples. I couldn't understand why American businessmen condemned these state enterprises. They were commercial firms. So it seemed to me that if they sold products in markets for a profit, they might as well be judged by the "bottom line," especially in the market economies of the West.

Two lucky breaks helped my investigation along. First, I received a grant to study American business performance in southern Italy. Because ENI and IRI (Istituto per la Ricostruzione Industriale, Institute for the Reconstruction of Industry) play such a large role in Italian business both as competitors and joint venture partners of American firms, I had to study these government enterprises too. I reported on their commercial dealings in my book *Managing Foreign Investments in Southern Italy* (Praeger, 1973). Second, I went to Ecuador—three times—as a consultant and Fulbright professor. Once I had to advise the local government on the organization and management of Cepe (Corporación Estatal Petrolera Ecuatoriana, Ecuadorian Petroleum State Corporation), the new government-owned petroleum firm, and how it might market its oil from the Amazon region.

In Italy and Ecuador, and later in Peru and elsewhere in Latin America, I collected data, analyzed them with the aid of my private enterprise background, and came up with recommendations. I thought that sovereignty was at bay, and the sooner local governments could copy American multinational firms, the better.

Well, I should have known better. My great history teacher, Arthur Preston Whitaker, who taught me Latin American history at the Wharton School, stressed the unique cultural history of the Spanish-speaking Latin American countries. My academic colleague, William Glade of the University of Texas at Austin, wrote a compelling economic history of this region stressing government intervention as the norm for change there. Multinational investment by privately-owned firms may contribute to economic development and change, but could never be its fundamental source. Frankly, ten years passed before I put these two insights together and began wondering about the applicability of the "received theory of American multinational investment" to regions of the world where governments intervene in the economy to create output for sale in domestic and foreign markets—something that much later I would label the "nexus."

Next I worked on building a data base for my general notion that sovereignty is not at bay. And again luck played a part. David Ewing came to the University of Alabama looking for new ideas for the *Harvard Business Review* and agreed to publish my first analytical piece on why American firms would have to learn how to do business with commercial state enterprises.

Responses to that article by businessmen suggested that there was a real need for better understanding of state enterprises and I decided to extend my research. I expanded the data bank GINSEM© (Giant Industrial State Enterprise Methodology) to its present fifty-nine state commercial enterprises. I read two decades of back issues of the *Financial Times* and other important foreign business publications. I interviewed many state enterprise executives.

Finally, I had what I was looking for: a coherent approach to state enterprises, their challenges to American firms, and the dangers they pose to the American business community.

I checked my calendar. It had taken three years to develop a theory, prepare a methodology, and test out my hypotheses.

Now I had to report my findings to my colleagues, hear their arguments, and refine my procedures. Another year went by.

I suppose I could say that I have been at this project for nearly a decade. Yet this book is simply a midpoint in my study of state intervention. A procession of protectionist measures, worries about resource scarcity, and alarms about the Kondratieff cycle call even the most skeptical American businessmen to demand federal intervention.

Will it come to pass that I will be able to buy Cheerios in a federal government food store? I pray that it won't happen here. For all our sakes.

Acknowledgments

My thanks to the many people who had an interest in seeing this book come to fruition. Huron Smith, a former graduate student, did yeoman service in preparing the numerical and computer analyses found in this book and in the series of professional papers prepared during 1976.

The international business faculty at the University of Wisconsin, especially Warren Bilkey, who read and commented on the last two drafts of the book, and Sol Levine, offered their classes as forums for testing out my theories and concepts.

The Academy of International Business and the Council of the Americas gave me a place on their annual programs to present my findings and to obtain reactions from professors and businessmen.

Douglas Walker, Ernest Ogram, and Morris Rosoff gave me useful advice from their viewpoints as businessmen, professor, and lawyer. Richard Lacey gave me invaluable comments about organization and presentation of materials. Other persons from the academic world and the business and legal communities as well as members of my family read one or more of the drafts. To all of these go my thanks.

Martin Kessler, vice-president and editor of Basic Books, gave me continuing encouragement during the four years it took to gather materials and write the book.

A special note of thanks to Janice, Katherine, Kristine, my parents, the Monks, and good friends who suffered silently while the book was in preparation.

DOUGLAS F. LAMONT
Chicago, Illinois

Foreign State Enterprises

Introduction:
The Foreign Summons

STATE ENTERPRISE CAPITALISM—the government acts as banker, owner, and manager of business firms—is a novel development for this country. Americans have traditionally assumed that private interests, by following their own instincts for profitable opportunities in foreign trade and investment, would secure America's rightful share of the world's resources.[1] But other nations saw things differently. They regarded privately-owned American multinational firms as challengers to their own economic independence, and they simply refused to compete under these rules.

Europeans have traditionally assumed that private interests, by closely adhering to the economic policies of government, would sustain Europe's position in international commerce. But instead of relying solely on their own privately-owned firms, which they protected and subsidized,

3

to meet this challenge, the French, Germans, and recently the British and Brazilians among others chose to establish government-owned, limited-liability business firms. Several of these firms exploited an advantage that less sophisticated state business firms had not enjoyed: their managers were equipped with financial, marketing, and personnel resources —and above all, relative freedom in decision making—to place their firms in the ranks of the multinational enterprises.

Today, there are fifty-nine state commercial enterprises[2] —12 percent of the "Fortune 500." And the trend is growing. Between 1957 and 1976, the number of such internationally competitive firms has increased twelvefold, while their sales have quadrupled every seven years and their assets have doubled every five years. These firms are now responsible for 21 percent of world sales for the 500 largest international business corporations headquartered outside the United States. And their sales and assets, as shown by their compound annual growth rates for the twenty-year period 1957 through 1976 and for the most recent period 1971 through 1976, are growing faster than similar privately-owned non-American business firms.*

This growth has enabled eleven foreign state enterprises to invest over $1 billion in acquiring American industrial firms. As we will show, these purchases are developments we cannot afford to ignore. Unchecked, they—together with an enormous and increasing number of foreign direct, real estate, and portfolio investments of all kinds—pose grave difficulties for the American economy within a decade. Like an iceberg in American shipping lanes, the state enterprises

* See chapters 2 and 7 and the Appendix for statistics.

4

are the most visible sign of a problem that is much more widespread and serious than it appears on the surface.

What signs of the iceberg are already apparent? Chapter 1 examines two major cases of direct investments in the United States by foreign state enterprises: how British Petroleum (BP) and Canada Development Corporation (CDC) took over Sohio and Texasgulf. Similar examples from developed and Third World countries underscore the subject of this book: how foreign governments have forged durable political and economic links with business firms to enable them to compete successfully in the open market— increasingly at American expense. The links range from tacit and temporary favoritism to public, explicit, and practically permanent contractual agreements. For example, 80 percent of French companies have entered into contracts with government, which regulates their pricing, investment, and export policies, in return for government business and easy credit. And Japanese firms regularly receive injections of debt capital from government development, industrial, and long-term credit banks to subsidize their export and foreign direct investment thrusts. The intention is to build the momentum and strength of this new form of political and economic competition swiftly before the American government and our private firms can grasp what is happening and regain their balance in the 1980s.

Of course, business and government interests are characteristically intertwined; both private and state-owned firms have often enjoyed special favors and privileges from their home governments, even in the United States. Until recently, though, such cozy relationships were typically informal, expedient arrangements rather than long-range mutual commitments. Often the relationships gave birth

5

to state enterprises too early, forcing them to disappear from the "Fortune 500" within two to three years.

What has evolved—over several decades, on-again, off-again—is a new form of government-business union which we call the *nexus*: a merger that is stable, effective, and affords each partner what it wants within clear, mutually-agreed boundaries. The strongest associations include the state enterprises as partners—especially the eight state multinationals*—and their energy businesses are the rapidly growing American subsidiaries. Bonded to them are the privately-owned firms that have entered into orderly marketing agreements with their home governments for the purpose of increasing the export content of industrial output and capturing foreign markets. Asymmetrical privilege for business firms is the unknown product of these unions we call the nexus.

Government-business linkage includes equity ownership (the state enterprise), rationalization of heavy industries (French schemes in the iron and steel, aluminum and chemical industries to regroup and merge firms), loans of debt capital for new investment (Japan, Inc.), and special tax favors to promote exports, foreign direct investments, and other commercial strategies favorable to the economic health of the nation-state. Foreign nexus intervention in the United States is a product of all of these. There is 1 billion dollars of foreign direct investment by state enterprises. Its sum is increased five times when the direct investment of government-supported privately-owned firms, such as France's Pechiney Ugine Kuhlmann and Japan's Mitsui, are added to this total. And when we understand how the

* See chapter 2 and Table 2–1.

6

investment capital of America's AMAX has been coopted to help them build market position here, it becomes apparent why this network of joint-venture contacts leads to a significant strengthening of French and Japanese economic power.

Throughout this book we will use the state enterprise as the example of nexus intervention because it is the most visible sign of the spread of industrial state enterprise capitalism through traditional international business strategies: acquisitions, local borrowing, domestic market penetration. When necessary to show a nuance important to Americans we will use the government-supported, privately-owned firms as an example of nexus intervention. Both types of government subsidized firms and the home government that owns and supports them have to put into place interrelationships based upon commercial autonomy for the firm and economic advantage to the nation-state. In this web of interlocking tax breaks, grants-in-aid, export subsidies, low cost direct investment loans, debt financing, and equity ownership, little thought is being given to the host country's preferences. A pattern of foreign direct investment is being replayed, but this time the beneficiaries are the foreign nation-state nexus and its government-subsidized business firms.

Commercially competitive state enterprises are both unfamiliar and formidable. By exporting to and investing in overseas markets, these firms can and do become multinationals. The changing roles that governments have played in their evolution, why they have chosen to compete in the American market, and why we should take specific steps to respond to them are the paths we follow to answer the question, "Is state capitalism in America's future?"

This book deals primarily with the expanding role of government-owned industrial firms as competitive corporations throughout the developed world. This includes the appropriation by the fifty-nine state enterprises of business functions reserved by law and historical practice to privately-owned firms. Western European governments and Canada, especially, faced with vigorous American competition overseas, together with growing political pressure to combat perceived threats to national sovereignty, have set up firms expressly to do battle with the American industrial giants in Europe, Third World nations, and even in the United States itself.

We pay special attention to the growth of the American subsidiaries. Until now, foreign state enterprises have acquired American industrial firms at will. Indeed, their right to do so has remained virtually uncontested. In 1973, the federal court in Houston ruled that it was up to Congress to pass legislation spelling out the limits of foreign government-owned business firms' freedom to do business in the United States. Without such laws, the court felt it had no choice but to let CDC take control over Texasgulf.

The precedents certainly were there. Only three and one-half years before, the Justice Department had permitted BP (British Petroleum) to take over Sohio, combine it with the British-owned Alaskan oil fields, and create a large integrated petroleum firm which could challenge even Exxon in the American market. Today, foreign state enterprises seeking to acquire American oil, coal, sulphur, potash, phosphate, and rubber tubing remain safe from State Department diplomatic pressures. Indeed, such pressure are rarely, if ever, seriously applied.

For nearly fifteen years, Americans did not pay much

attention to the European governments' drive for competitive market position in the United States. During that period, foreign state enterprises have successfully introduced in the American market such products as Total gasoline, DSM (Dutch State Mines) caprolactam, VW cars, and Motta desserts. So far, their challenge doesn't make headlines. The problem becomes more critical when we realize that 65 percent of their foreign direct investment is in petroleum and 33 percent is in minerals such as coal. And the ability of foreign state enterprises to raise capital from consortia of domestic banks, their freedom to take mineral leaseholdings on federal lands, their insistence on the right to hire and fire at will, and their invocation of "acts of God" clauses in contracts when supplies cannot be delivered to American buyers all signify that rights once available to privately-owned firms are now exercised by foreign governments and their business enterprises.

We have seen just the beginning of what could become an open season on the purchase of American resources and industrial firms. Clearly, such foreign direct investments —only the most visible form of the enormously increasing government-supported investments here—raise serious problems for the American business community.

The experience of competitive state enterprise investors in the United States illustrates an important truth about government's role in business: it works only when professional management, brought in from the private sector (for instance, American executives from privately-owned multinationals), is given a free hand to make strategic corporate decisions and then proceeds to exercise vigorous leadership. It is such leadership that has enabled many state enterprises to meet the American multinationals head-on with foreign direct investments of their own—particularly in the United States. These state enterprises have set up worldwide production and marketing systems that are able to guarantee high product quality, dependable supplies, and competitive prices.

Although their governments pass laws to restrict American access to oil in the North Sea and sulphur in Ontario, and to bar American purchase of locally-owned private firms, their enterprises thrive freely among us. For example, can it be said that the British and the Canadians are still within the bounds of reciprocity, as Congress intended in 1920, for petroleum, minerals, and rubber-mixing products? In its report, *Foreign Direct Investment in the United States*, the Department of Commerce suggests that they are not, and calls for corrective federal legislation.[3] We agree.

Two Challenges

Foreign governments and their state enterprises present us with two challenges. One is economic, the other political. We have yet to learn how to meet either of them, in part because they are intimately related and interdependent in the form of the nexus.

An economic challenge is apparent because they are attacking our market position abroad. We see in part one how CDC's takeover of Texasgulf was an explicit expression of Canadian policy to reduce American ownership of Canadian-domiciled petroleum and mineral resources. Polysar Limited, a CDC subsidiary, is buying up rubber-mixing plants in the United States to create a North American subsidiary large enough to reduce the American market share in Canada. British, French and German petroleum and coal investors are following suit, and Austrian and Brazilian state enterprise coal investors are taking options to buy up additional North American coal mines. Yet we still don't see this corporate strategy as a commercial threat, and the political side of the problem is even more elusive to the American public and American policy makers.

One reason is that we are so accustomed to parrying tactics that we haven't recognized that a strategy—much less a powerful one—is in force: the way state enterprises have systematically built their world-wide market position. As we see in part two, they have learned from their mistakes. Now, by abandoning domestic monopolies, by overturning myths about their ability to perform macroeconomic miracles, by adopting appropriate government intervention strategies, by going into joint ventures with government-supported private firms, and by becoming multinational firms, state enterprises have become truly competitive.

The strategy was not suddenly conceived in a government planning office. Had it abruptly appeared on the horizon like a flashy new machine, we wouldn't have mistaken it. But it evolved gradually over several decades, and we became so used to its various awkward preliminary forms that we paid no heed. Since the mid-1920s, when the French established CFP, other nations have gradually tied government to the very corporate fabric of a business firm. As we see in part three, by creating the government-state enterprise nexus, they forged regular home-host country foreign economic relationships without taking over the prerogatives of corporate management. After half a century, we have entered an "Age of State Enterprise Capitalism" in international business, a new form of competition for the American business firm.

The political challenge is equally serious—perhaps even more so because it is so hard to spot unless one knows how and where to look for it. Economic competition alone is not the problem; rather, it is the intent and methods of the political strategy employed in the United States and world-wide that give cause for concern. These nexus competitors are impairing our very ability to defend ourselves even when we finally choose to do so, not simply by building raw economic power, but by assuring its strength and resilience through political means.

In part four, we see how state enterprises are establishing a network of Wall Street bankers, Madison Avenue advertisers, and Washington lawyers. This group will soon have lobbying power to inhibit legislation restricting their efforts to control American energy resources and local consumer markets. Already, enterprise managers are using their American base to build up export markets in Latin America with all the special export-import benefits available to privately-owned American firms.

The Issue

All foreign state enterprise investors have worked with their home governments to restrict the freedom of our firms to invest in their home countries. Yet we unilaterally allow them to invest here without restriction. Because state enterprise direct investments are primarily in petroleum exploration and minerals extraction, it is especially urgent for the federal government to insist that foreign government-owned and government-supported firms can expect to receive only those rights that they are willing to grant our firms overseas —no more.

As we show in part five, the congressional policy of 1920 on reciprocity must not only be enforced; it must be amplified to apply beyond leaseholding, in order to deal with the broad scope of foreign direct investment by specially privileged firms. The precise connections between foreign direct investments and the nexus strategy are so complex and diverse that only a comprehensive federal policy such as the government's orderly marketing agreement with the steel industry will suffice.

Urgent as it is to understand the challenges, the evolution of the nexus, and the issues raised by the strategy, it is equally crucial not to react precipitously to foreign direct investments by state enterprises or to foreign direct investments in general. The solution is not to pass a stringent foreign investment review code as the Canadians did, which halts new investments. Rather, it is to demand reciprocity —to secure freedom for our firms to invest, for instance, in North Sea oil and Brazilian iron ore as a quid pro quo.

The "Age of State Enterprise Capitalism" has just begun. Were it not that the state multinationals and government-supported private firms are "Fortune 100" firms, the political result of the nexus' international business strategy would still be more like an ice floe than an iceberg. American firms could plow steadily through it rather than run aground. By isolating the largest state enterprises for study, we can clearly see the elements of political economy bonding government and business.

State enterprises form the visible tip of the iceberg. Their subsidized cousins from the private sector are the iceberg's underwater ram. The whole mass, most of it submerged, is the nexus itself. Its purpose is to compete at home, abroad, and in the United States and to use the world's capital funds, mineral resources, and manufacturing capacity and marketing connections to benefit particular nation-states.

Our sonar should guide us. When the British government offers subsidies to British Steel, when the European Common market develops an orderly marketing agreement for the European steel industry—these are warnings. The ties between government and enterprise are so firmly established in the political economy of nation-states that the nexus of power is impervious to traditional market forces.

It is time to help American business neatly and early circumvent this potential and unexpected danger. In doing so, we can reaffirm a tradition in our own history—one we tend to forget—in which both federal and state governments have acted with private business firms to accomplish critical national economic goals. If we fail to do so—either by sitting on our hands or by thrashing out unproductively —many more of our privately-owned business firms will link themselves up with foreign government-owned enterprises, for their foreign direct investments here are only a fraction of the pertinent nexus-related business activities in the United States.

Failure to detect the nexus danger now means that the 1980s will ring with cries of "Emergency! Reverse engines! Ready lifeboats!" as government-supported privately-owned firms and the nexus itself—which we believe to be four to six times larger than state enterprises—ram into the American economy. The energy and resources that would then be drained in struggling with the crisis would frustrate our other critical national goals for years.

14

PART ONE

Domestic Responses

1

America Has No Policy

ONLY FIFTEEN YEARS AGO, no foreign state enterprises had invested here. Indeed, privately-owned American firms could shrug off occasional weak challenges by Western governments to their overwhelming domination of the international economy. Yet amid pronouncements that the very sovereignty of these nations was at bay, foreign governments were busy transforming government-owned corporations into state multinational enterprises. Their mission: to control world resources, products, and markets. Aggressive worldwide, they are now determined to unseat us wherever our firms dominate local industries and to control American domestic markets in order to make the 1980s their decade rather than ours.

Foreign direct investments in America are an amazing story—all the more amazing because America has paid scant attention to it. More importantly, America is doing nothing to change the way the plot is developing.

Among the many examples of foreign investments here in recent years, two episodes show that America has no policy toward them: first, a consent decree in 1976, enabling BP to purchase a controlling interest in Sohio, and second, the 1973 purchase of Texasgulf by CDC.

BP is a state multinational enterprise with sales of $3.3 billion in 1968—the third largest industrial firm headquartered outside the United States. It wanted to expand in the United States by acquiring major petroleum companies here rather than building its own. Acquiring an operating firm usually permits a faster and cheaper way to expand than building refineries, marketing and distribution systems, and other commercial connections. In March 1969, BP bought Atlantic-Richfield-Sinclair properties and began negotiating for Sohio. In addition to the normal advantages for expansion, this purchase would open up new ways to finance the Alaskan pipeline.

The Justice Department may not have realized in late 1969, when the consent decree was being negotiated, how important the new economic power base for state enterprise capitalism was. However, it clearly had no intention of frustrating the plan, innocuous or not.

Any shift in federal policy towards direct investment by foreign state enterprises changes our foreign economic relations. The executive branch has been so determined to maintain the status quo that it has allowed foreign firms to concentrate economic power in ways that American firms are not permitted to use. The BP case is a prime example, for the 1950 Celler-Kefauver Amendment to Section 7 of the Clayton Act denied American members of the "Seven Sisters" petroleum cartel the ability to concentrate economic power through such massive mergers.

Indeed, Representative Celler had warned in the late 1960s that "British Petroleum is an instrumentality of the British government, giving the United States a reason beyond antitrust laws for intervening to prevent an eventual takeover of Sohio."

The consent decree confirmed the purchase of Atlantic Richfield-Sinclair properties, with two minimal concessions. BP had to sell off former Sinclair service stations in Pennsylvania competing directly with Sohio stations. Sohio had to sell enough stations in Ohio to reduce its business by 400 million gallons. BP thereby gained control of Sohio, its share expected to rise to 54 percent in 1979 as BP Alaskan oil is placed in the hands of Sohio. This domestic subsidiary now controls the nation's largest estimated domestic crude reserves (some 5.1 billion barrels) and a marketing system in twenty-one states.

The Justice Department did extract a token promise. As Sohio president Charles E. Spahr put it, the British government "has chosen not to interfere or impose its will in connection with commercial acts of BP. The potential is there, but the record is good." That is, even though the government owns 49 percent of BP, its role in company management is passive. He might have commented on what is and is not a commercial act, or who determines what is commercial, but he chose not to. Like most other American managers of new state enterprise subsidiaries, he put his best foot forward in an unknown situation. Fearing a disruption of favorable business conditions that might result from a major conflict between Congress and the executive over demands of foreign state enterprises to set up subsidiaries here, these spokesmen walk on eggs.

The second major episode happened in July 1973, when Texasgulf, Inc. tried to stop a takeover bid by CDC.

Texasgulf, which earned over two-thirds of its income from Canadian sources, also has multimillion-dollar American investments in potash mining in Utah, in phosphate mining in North Carolina, and in Pennsylvania and New York timber tracts. In giving the go-ahead for CDC to buy 10 million shares of Texasgulf, the court drew no distinction between foreign government and private investors because the President and the Congress had made no such distinction in the law.

Two years before, the Canadian Parliament had granted private commercial privileges to the wholly government-owned CDC, with these broad objectives:[1]

1. To create or develop Canadian businesses, resources, properties, and industries;
2. To expand and develop opportunities for Canadians to participate in the economic development of Canada through application of their skills and capital;
3. To invest in the shares of securities of any corporation owning property or carrying on business related to Canadian economic interests; and
4. To invest in ventures or enterprises, including the acquisition of property, likely to benefit Canada.

This plan typified the sophistication that state enterprises had developed since the 1950s, for CDC enjoyed wide latitude in management decision making in order to raise funds from both government and international sources.

Over two decades, European and Canadian state enterprises had learned how to improve domestic market management and counter threats of American investments. They had acquired a new mission: to compete against American firms in Third World markets and even to conquer American domestic markets. In 1971, this mission, supported by the priorities of the Trudeau government, gave the Canadians an aggressive model of government working hand-in-hand with business that transformed traditional United States-Canada economic relations in ways whose radical implications still pass almost unnoticed.

Within a year after its founding, CDC acquired Polysar Limited, a crown corporation, from the Canadian government, making CDC the owner of two important American industrial firms: Solar Chemical Corporation of Leominster, Massachusetts, and Polysar Latex of Chattanooga, Tennessee. It had created an integrated American rubber-mixing subsidiary. In the United States, it would gain experience, acquire additional plants, produce in volume, and keep unit costs down. In Canada, it would sell these low-cost products and use its influence in Ottawa to curtail further American investment in the rubber-mixing business there.

The federal court decision took no note of these changes in ownership and control. In fact, Judge Seals didn't even know about the plan to develop an integrated American rubber-mixing subsidiary which could become fully competitive both here and in Canada within a decade.

Among the pieces of conflicting advice that Judge Seals heard, the testimony of a distinguished Canadian law professor, Ivan R. Feltham of York University, is especially enlightening: "When there is a conflict between maximizing profits on behalf of the shareholders and acting in the best interests of Canada," he said, "the Canada Development Corporation's representatives on Texasgulf's Board of Directors must opt for doing what is best for Canadian national interests."[2]

Canadian-born economist John Kenneth Galbraith called this testimony "pure and self-serving nonsense,"[3] yet Feltham had expressed a sentiment that is widely- and deeply-felt in Canada. After experiencing years of increasing American control over their industries, Canadians felt victimized by an apparently imperial multinational economic order and were determined to fashion international enterprises that would be competitive worldwide but would be under the control of the Canadian government. Nothing was more crucial to this new policy than successful direct investments in the United States. Carl Beigie, executive director of Montreal's C. D. Howe Research Institute, explained the goal simply. Canada's plan, he said, is "to differentiate itself from the United States in a realistic, carefully organized manner."[4]

The decision of the Federal Court was a complete victory for Canadian government interests. Toronto's *Financial Post* headlined it: "The Judge went all the way—against Texasgulf."[5]

In his judgment, Judge Seals asked, "What should our national policy be in protecting the national interest of the American people from a real or an imaginary threat of the multinational corporation, regardless if it is a private foreign corporation but nevertheless is an instrument, directly or indirectly, of a foreign nation-state . . . such as Canada Development Corporation . . . British Petroleum . . . ?"

He answered his question this way: ". . . If the threat is real, it makes little difference if the foreign multinational is government-owned and -controlled or not. If it is government-controlled, at least we will know 'our enemy' and to whom it owes this allegiance and through diplomacy and treaties could balance their political influence and their economic power. . . ."

His conclusion: "Only the Congress or the executive branch has the resources to determine what is in the best interest of this country in the increasing problem of multinationals."[6]

In the 1970s, state enterprise performance at home, so indispensable to Canadian nationhood, has turned into a Dominion government-CDC challenge in the United States. The public development corporation—as apparently disparate direct investments have shown—has become an important North American investor and threatens to become an internationally competitive state enterprise in key growth sectors of the world economy.

Our commercial relationship with Canada is suddenly, unexpectedly, and permanently obsolete. The Canadian economic policy of using state enterprises to limit or take over American subsidiaries and to buy control over American corporations in the United States is unlikely to change. It has such deep visceral and emotional support among a broad spectrum of Canadians that we should consider it an accomplished fact.

Congress Requires Reciprocity

Such unilateral agreements as the CDC and BP deals are actually departures from our legal requirement of reciprocity in foreign economic policy. Over fifty years ago, in the

Mineral Leasing Act of 1920, Congress required that foreign nations be in a reciprocal commercial status with the United States. This means that once the executive branch finds that a nation's "laws, customs, and regulations" are being applied equally to American and national firms, American subsidiaries of their corporations can hold leases on federal lands. The insistence on reciprocity sprang from a concern to assure American firms a place in the world of British and European cartels. Congress doubtless hoped to spare America diplomatic tribulations like those that happened during the BP takeover of Sohio.

There is some evidence that the executive branch yielded to those pressures which Congress sought to avoid. As London's *Financial Times* bluntly put it: "European governments cannot be expected to maintain an open-door investment policy if European companies are restrained from mounting an effective challenge in the United States."[7] *Die Welt*, the influential West German newspaper, suggested America's roadblocks to British investment showed that the United States was a "closed shop." Even the French, who had always effectively nurtured their own domestic government-owned and -supported enterprises at the expense of American private investment in France, chimed in to aid their embattled European sister: "If a giant like British Petroleum isn't allowed to buy an American firm, what can smaller firms hope to achieve in the United States?"[8]

Faced by external forces, the executive branch failed to set guidelines to check the unfettered command and resulting political power a state multinational enterprise such as BP could bring to bear upon the United States. There is no evidence that in 1969 the executive branch seriously thought to ask for a new ruling on whether the United Kingdom was still in reciprocity with respect to petroleum. The attorney general's ruling of 1936 declared Great Britain reciprocal, but a 1948 update declared it *not* reciprocal with respect to coal, because coal had been nationalized under the National Coal Board. Presumably these rulings were considered sufficient to show how American firms were being treated by the British government.[9]

Today, the Department of the Interior refers all questions about reciprocity to the Department of State. To avoid offending foreign nations, the State Department has consistently interpreted reciprocity as liberally as possible. The resulting failure is to see no reason for finding Great Britain of Canada non-reciprocal. The Report to Congress on *Foreign Direct Investment in the United States* argues that the North Sea petroleum investment policies of Britain and the Foreign Investment Review Act of Canada deny similar commercial privileges to American firms. In effect, then, foreign state enterprises enjoy government privilege at the expense of privately-owned American firms.

Why America Needs a Policy

The executive branch has responsibilities to act and opportunities to set guidelines about leaseholdings on federal lands by foreigners. And where the law is silent on certain issues, the executive branch should submit legislation to set clear limits. These are minimal obligations. More broadly, America needs an explicit and enforced policy to clarify our economic philosophy—and what it must mean in practice —for other nations.

European and Canadian economic philosophy is unlike any that the American establishment and electorate would accept. The European idea of a cooperative and communal economy is reflected in national economic planning, rationalization (reorganization and integration) of industries, government-subsidized firms, and worker participation in management. In general, business firms serve society. Governments authorize spinoffs of privately held assets, recombinations into new corporations, and subsidies against all other businesses—foreign, domestic, government, private. But in practice, responsible governments depend on the private sector supported and subsidized by government to accumulate and allocate risk capital in the market.

Governments intervene in commercial activities because of national consensus. Britain nationalized industries; France established new state enterprises; Germany sold off noncontrolling interests in state enterprises to strengthen the private sector; France and Norway set up competing state enterprises; the United States and Italy assist failing private firms; Canada restricts foreign investment to help domestic enterprises. All seek lower prices and more dependable services. And all want business firms of international weight to serve domestic markets and compete overseas.

The Europeans contend that government, for the sake of national sovereignty, must intervene to protect the nation-state against American multinational firms. Otherwise, how can it legitimately dominate the nation's political, economic, and cultural life?

The antecedents of state enterprise capitalism show how

strong a hold the idea has on Europeans. State enterprise capitalism was an attractive idea as far back as 1913, when Winston Churchill spoke to Parliament about British Petroleum (then called Anglo-Persian Oil): "We must become owners, or at any rate controllers, at the source of at least a proportion of the supply of natural oil which we require." And in 1914 he told Parliament that the government would buy a 51 percent share of the corporation to assure the Navy and the Empire oil at a price not controlled by Royal Dutch Shell.[10] But the government would not, as Sohio's Spahr reminded us sixty years later, "impose its will in connection with commercial acts."

A decade later, France decided to act. Starting with the notion that the Anglo-American cartel could control the French domestic oil market, France took Germany's 23.75 percent interest in Turkish Petroleum Company (later Iraq Petroleum) in First World War reparations, turning it into Cie. Francaise des Pétroles (CFP) in 1924.

The passing years have shown the weakness of intervention. Logical as intervention seems in the beginning, there is often no logical end to it. As British economist Peter Bauer points out, the current British economic sickness "is to be found in the inadequate return on capital, not in insufficient (government) spending."[11] British coal, steel, and oil industries and British Leyland and Chrysler Corporation automobiles are nationalized, controlled by state enterprises, or subsidized by the government. Italian state enterprises compete over the remains of failing private firms. The IRI conglomerate has become a virtual state within a state, subject only to its ability to exclude foreign and domestic competition from its protected domestic market.

27

Other Europeans, having learned the limitations of government intervention, let their state enterprises compete for resources and markets. To combat American multinationals, they force foreign investors to take domestic firms as partners, to share technologies, and to invest in depressed regions. While they borrowed the single-supplier state monopoly corporate structure from the British and the conglomerate state enterprise corporate structure from the Italians, they also created domestic competition among state enterprises and between them and government-supported private firms. Norway, Germany, Spain, Canada, and now Britain are following the French practice of creating two or more state enterprises in the same industry. Where state enterprises cannot do the tasks needed in petrochemicals, steel, and aluminum, Europeans have combined state and private enterprises, both foreign and domestic. Finally, they have forced their business enterprises to support the balance of payments by expanding exports and increasing foreign direct investments.

As CDC and BP illustrate, government intervention in the economy has become flexible; it is not hampered by dominant socialist doctrines or by state enterprises so powerful that they can insulate themselves from market competition. If government cannot improve industrial performance by its volume of investment, and if centralized decision making is too rigid to adapt, the French version of state enterprise capitalism and its Canadian, Norwegian, and German derivatives show the way to success.

As Leonard Silk points out, the market may not be an adequate opponent to organized government economic power. Combat through cartels, monopolizing of supply channels, state bargaining, and central planning may doom the market itself.[12] No one can be certain how foreign and domestic government intervention in the American economy will develop. But unless we understand what is going on in the international economy, we will hand over foreign economic power to foreign state enterprise capitalism.

Ironically, we will do so in the name of the free market economy.

2

Facing the Two Challenges

"THE FORTUNE DIRECTORY of the 500 Largest Industrial Corporations Outside the United States" lists fifty-nine foreign government-owned business enterprises; their annual sales are at least $395 million. Almost three-quarters of them are completely government-owned; the others are controlled through government ownership of 10 percent or more of their equity shares. Practically all are domestically competitive. Some, like Vale do Rio Doce of Brazil, are supported by mandated joint-venture partnerships in new foreign direct investments.

Types of State Enterprises

The fifty-nine enterprises fall into three major categories according to their role in international business (Table 2–1).

State multinational enterprises are government-owned business firms with foreign direct investments in Western Europe, North America, and Third World countries. With 20 percent of their production capacity, volume of sales, or number of employees located outside their home countries, they are like privately-owned multinational firms.

Eight firms are state multinationals. It is primarily the astonishing success of these firms that forces the United States to establish a policy of reciprocity in foreign investment.

Another thirty-two enterprises form the second major category, firms which are not multinationals but engage in international business:

Five are *potential multinationals*. They have made important foreign investments, have created a significant volume of exports and imports, and have well-defined managerial strategies for becoming state multinationals.

Two Brazilian enterprises show that less developed countries can transform single-supplier monopolies into internationally competitive firms. Their recent success in expanding trade and overseas investments confirms that state enterprise capitalism is an important way to organize economic relations among countries in the southern as well as the northern hemisphere.

Fourteen other state enterprises are *important internationals* because of their foreign trade, but they have not made enough foreign direct investments or created a useful international managerial system to qualify as potential mul-

TABLE 2-1

Fifty-nine State Enterprises*

I.   State Multinational Enterprises (8)
    1. British Petroleum
    2. Dutch State Mines
    3. Elf-Aquitaine
    4. Ente Nazionale Idrocarburi
    5. Compagnie Française des Pétroles
    6. Montedison
    7. Renault
    8. Volkswagenwerk

II. State Enterprises Engaged in International Business (32)
    A. Potential Multinationals (5)
        9. Norsk Hydro
        10. Petrobrás
        11. Statsföretag
        12. Vale do Rio Doce
        13. Veba (includes Gelsenberg)
    B. Important Internationals (14)
        14. Alfa Romeo
        15. Bharat Heavy Electrical
        16. British Leyland
        17. Dalmine
        18. Enpetrol
        19. Gelsenberg (without Veba)
        20. Iscor
        21. Italsider
        22. Seat
        23. Rolls Royce
        24. Ruhrkohle
        25. Saarbergwerke
        26. Salzgitter
        27. Viag
    C. Petroleum Single-supplier Monopolies From Producing Countries (3)
        28. National Iranian Oil Company
        29. Pemex
        30. Petróleos de Venezuela
    D. Other Single-supplier Monopolies (10)
        31. British Steel
        32. Charbonnages de France
        33. Codelco
        34. Entreprise Minière et Chimique
        35. National Coal Board
        36. OMV
        37. Siderurgica Nacional
        38. Sidor
        39. Vöest-Alpine
        40. Zimco

III. Domestic State Enterprises (19)
    41. Aerospatiale
    42. Astilleros Espanoles
    43. Butano
    44. Cepsa
    45. Chinese Petroleum
    46. Ensidesa
    47. Enso-Gutzeit
    48. Indian Oil
    49. Morinaga Milk Products
    50. Neste
    51. Petroliber
    52. Seita
    53. Semperit
    54. SIBP
    55. SNECMA
    56. Steel Authority of India
    57. Steyr-Daimler-Puch
    58. Tabacalera
    59. Turkiye Petrolleri

*Note: All information in this book about state enterprises is extracted from the author's State Enterprise Data Bank. These fifty-nine largest state enterprises form the corpus of the author's Giant Industrial State Enterprise Methology (GINSEM©) which is an analytical methodology for comparing the performance of state enterprises and private firms (by industry, country, and geographic region) and for comparing the performance of alternative sets of state enterprises (by industry, country, and geographic region) among themselves. The results of these analyses are presented throughout the book and are summarized in Tables A-1 through A-14 in the Appendix.

Source: "The Fortune Directory of the 500 Largest Industrial Corporations Outside the United States," *Fortune*, August 1977, pp. 226-35.

tinationals. Their relative failure internationally, particularly in the United States, is an instructive contrast to the bounding success of the thirteen multinationals and potential multinationals.

The three *petroleum single-supplier monopolies from the producing countries* have sufficient petroleum reserves and sales volume to become internationally competitive. Other members of OPEC would support their drive for a position in the international market, but first their home countries must follow Brazil's lead and free them from bureaucratic constraints. The National Iranian Oil Company is the one to watch most closely as it expands rapidly at the expense of the "Seven Sisters" and their European petroleum state enterprise counterparts.[1]

Ten other *single-supplier monopolies* have sufficient ore reserves or domestic manufacturing capacity and sales volume to become internationally competitive once their governments remove bureaucratic restrictions. Without a strong OPEC-type organization supporting them, though, their sales volume and profitability depend upon international price fluctuations and they won't give up their government subsidies.

Nineteen are *domestic state enterprises*. Their international business activities are marginal, and they are also unwilling to sacrifice their subsidies even when doing so is the first step towards becoming fully competitive at home.

Finally, several government-supported privately-owned firms are receiving injections of government equity capital (e.g., Chemische Werke Huls, F. Krupp, Poclain, and Granges) sufficient to make them state enterprises. And another 230 firms, such as France's Saint-Gobain-Pont-à-Mousson and Japan's Hitachi, have special contracts with

33

the home governments regulating their export and foreign direct investment policies in return for low-cost loans, special tax breaks, and government business. In short, over 50 percent of the "Fortune 500" business firms have a privileged status in the international economy not now available to American firms.

Phenomenal Growth in Sales

One-eighth of the "Fortune 500," or the fifty-nine enterprises produced one-fifth of the sales in 1976 (Table A–1 in Appendix). Their sales totaled $185,431,718,000 at the end of 1976 versus sales totaling $709,689,720,000 for privately-owned, non-United States firms—a ratio of 1 to 4 of all listed corporations. And the gap gets smaller each year. Both the number of state enterprises and their share of exports and domestic sales will increase even faster. Between 1957 and 1976 their number has increased twelvefold, their sales have quadrupled every seven years, and their assets have doubled every five years. This is the minimum rate to be expected through the mid-1980s.

A minor reason for this high projection is that *Fortune* does not list some state enterprises, such as Polysar, whose sales exceed $395 million, either because of data problems or because *Fortune* doesn't know about them. A second reason is that the heart of our argument: governments in the developed world are taking over privately-owned assets explicitly to compete with American multinationals.

New state enterprises will not follow the pattern of the older ones, which emerged when private firms collapsed as transportation and utilities revenues fell or governments introduced socialist experiments. Instead, as the 1975 appearance in *Fortune* of Norsk Hydro and Vale do Rio Doce illustrate, governments join their national business communities to renew firms they believe can become state multinationals. For example, Mexico recently merged its three major steel producers into a new holding company, Sidemex. Fresh capital will enable Sidemex facilities in Monterrey to produce the high-quality steels needed to bring Mexico's new petroleum and natural gas discoveries to market in the United States.[2] France is using a similar strategy to revitalize its steel industry and make it competitive on a world-wide basis.

International Private Capital Support

The need for international capital and for knowledgeable managers makes mixed ownership particularly attractive. For example, in 1975 Norsk Hydro sold $40 million in bonds to Hambros Bank Ltd. and others, and in 1976 it sold DM 100 million in bonds to Deutsche Bank, Commerzbank, and others; and in 1975 London Multinational Bank and others loaned Vale do Rio Doce $45 million; in 1976 it too sold DM 70 million in bonds to Dresdner Bank and others.[3]

These injections will speed the growth of these firms far faster than governments could by making additional tax revenues available. The international private banks make certain that a new generation of state enterprises will become truly multinational during the 1980s, for governments which

35

maintain a consistent policy of national control coupled with managerial independence regarding commercial decisions will benefit from the faith of the international financial community.

Although *Fortune* is the best source of comparative international data on state enterprises, some of the fifty-nine firms have published inadequate records, or their data are thought to be influenced by government pressures. In these cases, the international financial community requires the national government to guarantee new loans unconditionally. Furthermore, firms from countries with large balance-of-payments deficits and intractable socio-political problems are considered high credit risks and will be at a disadvantage. For instance, when the Italian 1974 balance-of-payments showed a $10 billion deficit, European banks were chary of lending funds to Italy's nationalized industries and treated the profit-making $7.2 billion ENI to no better terms than the loss-ridden Italian railways.[4]

Labor Force

Since 1963, state enterprises have consistently employed about 16.5 to 17 percent of the total labor force for the largest industrial corporations outside the United States, and the number of employees is bound to grow. For example:

1. In 1962, when the *Fortune* directory listed 200 firms, nineteen state enterprises employed 1.3 million people.
2. In 1971, when *Fortune* listed 300 firms, thirty-six state enterprises employed 2.2 million.
3. Currently, *Fortune* lists fifty-nine firms employing 3.3 million (Table A–13 in Appendix).

State enterprises' employees may become as common in North America as they are today in Northern and Mediterranean Europe.

Assets Double every Five Years

As table A–10 (in the Appendix) shows, the assets of the state enterprises in the *Fortune* series have doubled every five years from 1957 (2.4 billion dollars) to 1976 (173.2 billion dollars). With about .65 percent (1.14 billion dollars) of their assets invested in American subsidiaries, these enterprises are barely beginning to become important new sources of jobs, tax revenues, and market share competition for American firms here.

Economic, political, and cultural unknowns may change the projections, but they will not change the trend. In fact, high rates of inflation or unemployment or some combination of the two that Western nations can't control could fuel government's desires to own the key capital-hungry industrial sectors of the international economy. The United States cannot affect the development of new state enterprises—their asset build-up or their command over world supply channels for oil and other natural resources—merely by holding out against state enterprise capitalism at home. In the next ten years the United States must decide what to do about direct investments by these firms. We needn't look far for specific evidence, for that $200 million investment by Volkswagenwerk in New Stanton, Pennsylvania will encourage France's Peugeot and other government-supported automobile firms to invest here also or lose international competitiveness.

Having One's Cake and Eating It Too

There's nothing wrong with foreign direct investments as long as governments don't exercise undue commercial control over their business corporations, but three issues of reciprocity are already apparent.

The first concerns the BP-Sohio control over Alaskan oil. American oil firms must sell 51 percent of their North Sea production to British National Oil Corporation (BNOC) and give it a majority voice on their operating committees.[5] Moreover, under the British government's "full and fair" opportunity agreement, BP and BNOC must buy their underwater steel pipe from a sister state enterprise, the British Steel Corporation, rather than from competing foreign firms.[6] The British view their North Sea policies and related supply contracts as purely domestic matters. We should not.

The second issue concerns mergers of state enterprises to concentrate economic power in the United States. The Clayton Act prohibits the type of concentration that the French accomplished in 1976 by merging Elf-Erap and Société nationale des pétroles d'Aquitaine in France, Canada, and the United States.[7] The newly-merged parent firm, the $6 billion corporation called Elf-Aquitaine—the newest "sister" of the international oil cartel—is free to reorganize its $81.5 million investment in the United States so that its American subsidiary can help meet long-term corporate objectives.

Elf-Aquitaine's activities in the United States include:

1. a 5 percent interest in the Oil Shale Corporation ($2.4 million, 1964);

2. a 92 percent interest in Westrans Industries ($54 million, 1975);
3. the oil, gas, and mineral properties of Pruett & Hughes valued at $35 million, 1975;
4. 100 percent of Towne, Paulsen & Co. (for undisclosed amounts, 1975);
5. 100 percent of M&T Chemicals (for undisclosed amounts, 1977).[8]

In Canada, Elf-Aquitaine's investments include Banff Oil Limited (for $21.5 million) and Elf Oil Exploration and Production (for $20.6 million).[9]

Except for the investment in Towne, Paulsen & Co., a marketer of prescription generic drugs, all the rest of Elf-Aquitaine's investments in the United States are managed by its subsidiary in Alberta, Canada, and are in the petroleum and natural gas industries. Its American assets (Mississippi natural gas, Pennsylvania coal, and oil shale reserves in many northwestern states and the Gulf Coast) are of sufficient quality that Smith Barney, Harris Upham & Co. and Kuhn Loeb & Co. were able in 1976 to place $50 million in notes for Elf-Aquitaine U.S.A., Inc. without requiring the French government to guarantee this credit extension.[10]

In the United States, the French petroleum state multinational enterprises behave as if they are privately-owned, with no French government link. Most visible is CFP, in which the French government holds a 40 percent controlling interest.

In 1966, CFP pioneered the approach of going into Wall Street and buying the stock of American corporations. It bought one-third of Leonard Refineries of Alma, Michigan for $6,839,591, and in 1970 it paid $12.6 million more for the remaining shares.[11] Leonard became another wholly-owned subsidiary of French state enterprise capitalism managed from Alberta.

Meanwhile, the French-owned Total Petroleum (North America), Limited bought Martin Oil Services, with service stations in Illinois and Wisconsin, and Citrin Oil Company, with service stations and a refined products terminal in Detroit, for undisclosed amounts.[12] In 1976, Total took over Hanover Petroleum Corporation for $35 million to control an important new source of Texas crude.[13] All told, an investment of some $54.4 million between 1966 and 1976 created an integrated petroleum operation in the United States.

Through Total Petroleum (North America) CFP was free to pursue its own commercial interests in the United States without any guidance or restraint from the federal government, something the French government won't permit American firms to do. Both CFP and Elf-Aquitaine pose substantive questions about reciprocity in France for American oil firms. Yet the American government, anxious to please, does not raise them.

The third issue concerns the Japanese quest for dominance in high-technology electronics.[14] Through the Very Large Scale Integration Program, the Japanese government is lending $250 million to its sem conductor and computer firms to buy American processes, manufacturing techniques, and components. The Japanese are free to acquire American personnel, resources, and microtechnology firms although similar entry strategies by American firms in Japan are blocked by government administrative regulations and strict control over provision of debt capital by government developmental, industrial, and long-term credit banks. Moreover, while AT&T is free to buy Japanese components, the Japanese government forbids the domestic telecommunications monopoly from buying foreign components. The rules are different. We need to insist on equal and fair treatment of both countries' products in each other's countries. Since Japanese government-supported privately-owned firms make up about one-fifth of the "Fortune 500"—and a large portion are within the top "100"—these government-directed commercial actions in high-technology electronics, aluminum, steel, and chemicals force us to demand answers to the questions posed by reciprocity. No amount of negotiation over the reduction of tariff barriers will make the changes needed in Japanese practices towards the American market.

Alienation of American Resources

Many foreign state enterprises alienate key American resources without challenge—their use of Alaskan oil, Utah potash, and West Virginia coal is for them to determine.

In 1974, for instance, the Hugo Stinnes unit of Veba—a potential multinational—and Ruhrkohle, another German state enterprise, paid $24 million for a 900,000-ton per year coal producer in West Virginia and Kentucky. This coal is now being shipped to West Germany to fuel its electrical generators.[15] By 1977, British state enterprises held 49.2 percent of total foreign state enterprise investment here. Canadian firms were second with 31.2 percent; French firms held 15.6 percent; West German firms held 2.8 percent; and Dutch firms ranked fifth with 1.2 percent. These figures don't include investments for undisclosed amounts of German leasing investments to recondition railroad boxcars.

State enterprises prefer to invest in oil and natural gas industries. From 1962 to 1977, BP, CFP, and Elf-Aquitaine invested over $563.9 million to buy American firms—65 percent of state enterprise direct investments here.*

Their second preference is to invest in natural resources such as phosphate and coal. CDC and Veba invested over $280 million—32 percent of total state enterprise investments.

Their third preference is investment in production of fertilizers, caprolactam, latex, and other products. CDC and DSM invested over $55 million—3 percent.

Investments in all three categories are understated, but the manufacturing sector reports more state enterprises investing for undisclosed amounts. For example, Veba's machinery subsidiary, Hugo Stinnes, owns American Drill Brushing Co. and Richard Brothers Punch Co. Other West German firms, such as the steel firm Salzgitter, which owns American Pecco Steel and Feralloy Corporation, have investments here too. Germany's aluminum state enterprise, Vaw (Vereinigte Aluminium-Werke), owns the Channel Master aluminum plant at Ellenville, New York.[16] And there are more. Since 1968, foreign direct investments in American firms by state enterprises have been near 3 percent or more of the total foreign direct investment. And similar investments by government-supported private firms raise that figure by a factor of four.

The real issue is not whether foreign state enterprises invest here; it is what types of investments they make and

* Calculations by author.

under what conditions. Present rules permit any type of investment under conditions set by the investor. They include no place for the federal government to make the public interest felt. The executive branch, Congress, business and labor, and above all the general public must understand how double-edged the character of foreign direct investment is: on the one hand, it has become an important resource to the health of the nation's economy; on the other hand, through its nexus ties, it is a potential danger to the market itself.

Reciprocity for Direct Investments: A Policy Goal

The shift to an international economy in which the government acts as a "merchant banker" calls for our full understanding of what others are doing to attack our market position. We face competitive state enterprises whose commercial power flows directly from their multinational status, close links to home governments, and the success of their American subsidiaries. Our grasping of these three important facts brings us to one conclusion: the need to reinvigorate Congress' policy on investment reciprocity.

When the 1920 reciprocity law is applied against foreign firms whose governments give them preference over American firms, it is effective. In the early 1920s we denied public land leases to Royal Dutch Shell because American oil firms could not purchase new concession areas in the Netherlands East Indies. The colonial government ceased giving concession preferences to Dutch firms, and we lifted our embargo on federal leaseholdings.

Since foreign state enterprises and government-supported privately-owned firms—this nexus of international commercial power—seek to control key American resources and markets, we need to do the same thing today. The reciprocity law must be broadened to include solutions to the growing number of attacks on our market position by the North Sea petroleum investment policies of Britain, the Foreign Investment Review Act of Canada, the exclusionary laws of Japan and Brazil, and similar legislation elsewhere in the world.

Given the great commercial strength of the fifty-nine state enterprises and the fact that 234 of the "Fortune 500" privately-owned, non-American firms are linked by tariff protection, subsidies, cheap money loans, and other special preferences to their home governments, a second policy option may have to be introduced to support policies of investment reciprocity: orderly marketing agreements. European governments use these today to shelter their steel state enterprises and privately-owned steel firms from the onslaught of Japanese competition. Through such agreements rationalization schemes are being introduced, particularly in France, to modernize plant and equipment and to bring a better balance of iron and steel production between the older areas of Alsace-Lorraine and the newer area of production at Fos-sur-Mer on the Mediterranean. Such orderly marketing agreements permit British Steel and Italy's Finsider to concentrate their attention on building up service centers in the United States to finish and sell mill products at prices that compete well with those of American steel fabricators. Because of these nexus arrangements, the federal government has had to set up a scheme of reference prices—one type of orderly marketing agreement—to reduce the Japanese and European threat to employment in the steel industry.

Will a policy of investment reciprocity and orderly marketing agreements work against the international commercial power of the government-state enterprise-privately-owned foreign nexus? Are the European and Japanese government-business relationships too strong to be countered by these two defensive weapons? Should we have ready an offensive tactic as well?

Revolutionary as the creation of state enterprises out of our own government funds—public taxes—must seem, we need to consider it not only as a last resort when big corporations fail (e.g., the Penn Central), but when large foreign government-owned corporations seek to make foreign investments that attack our market position. It is fashionable in American business today to show all government as the bumbling manager who can't deliver the mail on time. This is nonsense. Such condemnation forgets how state governments built canals and railroads during the pre-Civil War years, how the federal government managed a petroleum business during the Second World War, how today the two Dakotas operate profit-making flour mills and cement businesses, and how the federal government runs passenger and freight railroads. There have been modest efforts of state enterprise capitalism throughout our history. But until recently these domestic varieties of state enterprise capitalism were rare exceptions.

The idea that government owners of state enterprises in turn pick their management teams also seems extraordinary as an option for the United States, yet this country did exactly that when it established Amtrak and Conrail. At the same time as the federal government has become the banker, owner, and manager of American railroad state enterprises, no one in government nor in these two railroad enterprises has thought very deeply about the nature of government control over American state enterprise.

The time has come to consider this and many other problems. If the United States does not prepare itself with answers, in twenty years it may find that like the British it had invested its capital funds unwisely in businesses with low productivity and yields. Since state enterprise capitalism is earning a place in the national economy as it did elsewhere in the Western world, the best strategy is to ensure that it contributes to our national economic well-being.

The vast literature on multinational firms deals with privately-owned firms and their problems. The Department of Commerce prepared its report to the Congress on *Foreign Direct Investment in the United States* between 1974 and 1976. Yet the report hardly mentions the impact of direct investments by foreign state enterprises upon the petroleum and minerals industries, and it shows no concern for how state enterprises and other government-subsidized firms could alter the government-business relationship within our national market economy.

The state enterprise achievement to date is little noticed in the United States, even among American advocates of more national economic planning. They do not recognize, for instance, that the sale of American coal producers to Veba and Charbonnages de France (CDF, French Coal Mines) and Italsider links these American businesses to a foreign political power. They never ask the fundamental question: how do foreign governments use state enterprises to strengthen their economies? Even astute observers of Canadian-American relations do not understand Polysar's plans for the United States, let alone its intention to drive American producers from the Canadian market. Indeed, no American who favors a stronger role for government in meshing business plans with national economic plans has seen the other side of the coin—the stronger role of foreign governments in shaping state enterprise policies, the weaker the position of American firms in the international economy.

Advocates of national economic planning fail to see that if the United States permits direct investment by foreign state enterprises to continue, it should provide the American economy with maximum economic benefits. The United States cannot permit the wilful use of multinational plans to disrupt our economy—for example, DSM's insistence that its Augusta, Georgia caprolactam plant supply its English buyers rather than its American buyers after its caprolactam plant in England burned. Right now, the federal government has no legal mechanism to insist that foreign state enterprise do anything.

47

PART TWO

How State Enterprises
Became Multinationals

ALTHOUGH Western industrial state enterprise capitalism was conceived in the early post-Second World War years, it was not born until firms became commercially-run industrial enterprises. Only when government was no longer intent on regulating business, but rather intervened in the economy to promote an orderly market, did the fundamental relationship between government and business mature. In turn, business accepted government's tutelage: government terminated crown corporations, denationalized industries, and sought new ways to force their enterprises to compete worldwide without losing control of them.

The range of relationships between government and state enterprise is as wide as the cultural chasms which separate the countries that have introduced state enterprise capitalism into their national economies. There are, however, three major ways in which governments control state enterprise management: the initial British position of noninterference; the Third World method of direct and continuous intervention; and the French insistence that commercial decisions support national economic policy.

Although the British no longer follow a laissez faire policy, the Netherlands and Germany still follow the practice. For instance, the government nominates all members of the DSM's board of directors but stays out of corporate decision making.[1] Since the early 1960s when it charged the company to close obsolete mines, to enter the natural gas and petrochemical businesses, and to become competitive in Europe, the Dutch government has kept hands off.[2] Germany follows the old British model except in the petroleum industry, for the West German government controls and directs Veba.[3]

At the other extreme is the Third World's mixture of state enterprise capitalism and Fabian socialism. Government-owned corporations do not have a free hand to take risks, allocate capital, or set market prices within national and international markets. For example, some single-supplier state enterprises are given monopoly powers at home, yet they must promote national economic development without joint venture help from privately-owned international firms. Spain in the 1960s and Brazil in the 1970s have tried to purge themselves of these mistakes. Both Spain's Instituto Nacional de Industria and its many subsidiaries, and Brazil's Petrobrás and Vale do Rio Doce have flourished as their governments loosened control.

Canada, Norway, Sweden, Austria, Spain, South Africa, Brazil, and other countries throughout the Western world follow the French model. Although under way for over thirty years, it became visible only when governments actively rationalized industries and began setting oil, petrochemical, and minerals policies requiring state enterprises to combine private and public financial resources with managerial expertise in order to make industries competitive worldwide. In 1962, the change could already be predicted but had not taken place. By 1978 it had become an accomplished fact.

Governments may be unable completely to rid themselves of single-supplier monopolies, to grant management sufficient autonomy, or to control their state enterprises once they become multinational firms. These are problems to be worked out as state enterprises move from being protectors of domestic capitalism to competitors in world markets. As we shall see, their drive to build up market position worldwide means the age of state enterprise capitalism is still very much in its infancy.

3

Why State Monopolies Failed

AFTER the Second World War, the Europeans tried to control key extractive industries by authorizing single-supplier monopolies for coal, iron and steel, and potash to mine ore regardless of profit or loss. At the same time, governmental ministries could close mines, change labor routines, and raise prices.[1] Of course, firms could not independently manage mining or sales to recover costs, because governments intervened in day-to-day scheduling and pricing decisions. After repeated failures, some governments recognized that state monopolies merely fed the controlled sector, where taxes subsidize prices, new venture capital, managerial salaries, and dividends returned to government.

Legacies of the Second World War

The prospect in the late 1940s of Russian communism taking over the war-torn European countries was hypothetical. But the prospect in the 1950s and 1960s of democratic socialism gaining power was real. European public opinion was deeply divided over how the economy should be organized. After the communist takeover of Czechoslovakia, governments actively used state-owned monopolies and other noncompetitive business entities to discourage domestic communists from calling for totalitarian excesses in Italy and France. Following Scandinavian examples, Britain nationalized coal and steel industries through the ballot box, despite American distrust for such economic experiments.

In 1949, West Germany began to unsnarl the tangled ownership of Nazi properties by dividing them up between the new Federal Republic of Germany and its constituent länder (states). Portions of four major government business entities, Veba (coal, electricity, and chemicals), Salzgitter (steel, coal, and heavy machinery), Viag (aluminum, mining, and electricity), and Volkswagenwerk (automobiles and trucks) were put on the block. By 1959, the Bonn government had sold $20 million worth to private German interests—one percent. Two years later the government sold all but 20 percent of its shares in Volkswagenwerk in the open stock market, but decided not to follow completely the free enterprise model of America. Instead, Bonn retained control of 72 percent of aluminum, 44 percent of zinc, 40 percent of lead, 34 percent of iron ore, 26 percent of hard coal, 17 percent of crude oil, 16 percent of shipbuilding, 15 percent of electricity, 5 percent of ingot steel, and 5 percent of pig iron.[2]

Italians were even less enthusiastic about dismantling their conglomerate relic of the fascist era, the IRI. With European Coal and Steel Community funds they phased out or modernized coal mines, iron mines and steel mills.[3] By 1951, the IRI's 300 subsidiaries and the new Italian single-supplier for petroleum, ENI, competed in the Western market economy. Finally, a coalition of Christian Democrats and Socialists confirmed government's right to use these firms to promote economic development in Italy's depressed southern region.

The French held rigid views on government's right of tutelage. That is why they had directed CFP to take control of 25 percent of France's domestic petroleum market and established single-supplier monopolies for the domestic production of coal and potash.[4]

While German and Italian enterprises used European Coal and Steel Community funds to close mines or increase productivity, the Dutch carried the process one step further. They used the funds to close mines and retrain workers for jobs in new businesses with great growth potential in the world economy.[5] The French rejected this strategy in the 1950s, insisting on single-industry solutions, but reversed themselves many years later after wasting billions of francs.

British nationalization of steel in 1946, coupled with the establishment of the National Coal Board, signalled an early and substantial decline in Europe's concern for American views on how national economies should be organized. When the Conservative government sold British Steel Corporation to British private interests in 1951, no amount of cajoling could make do with antiquated plant and equipment and noncompetitive work rules, and the corporation faced certain renationalization once Labour returned to power. That happened in 1967.

The British Steel Corporation experience, the sale of Volkswagenwerk shares to the German public in 1961, and Labour's sale of British Petroleum shares in 1966 confirm an important conclusion: governments must turn business entities into profit-making state enterprises with a long-term future before selling portions of them to private interests which will sustain and nurture them.

American warnings about the spread of socialism were unavailing. Americans saw state monopolies as the ruination of multilateralism, free trade, and free enterprise. By setting up single-supplier monopolies in coal, iron and steel, potash, shipyards and ship construction, etc., Europe had shown how state monopolies might tear gaping holes in America's preference for a free and open international economy. In these early years, they were unable to do so only because they failed to make these business entities competitive and profitable at home.

In Europe, these firms, challenged by American multinationals, supposed themselves as repelling an invasion of foreign capital. State monopolies stampeded governments into restricting the flow of foreign direct investments to avoid a head-to-head contest between the multinationals and the state monopolies. All told, these entities were business failures. They took large shares of public revenues and returned few dividends or lower prices.

Simon Nora Calls for Reform

In November 1968, Simon Nora, as chairman of a French government working group, made his celebrated and prescient attack on government subsidies of state monopolies and other forms of noncompetitive, government-owned business entities. He made four major points.[6]

1. Between 1945 and 1966, West Germany had built state enterprises which were larger and more profitable than similar French firms.[7]

For example, Renault, a wholly-owned French government state enterprise, was then only one-third the size of Volkswagenwerk, in which the Federal Republic held a 20 percent share. Renault's return on investment was only one-fifth Volkswagenwerk's

Nora also indicted the government subsidies of coal (50 percent, or 2.5 billion francs), for even though the firm's internally generated capital declined to almost nothing, still the French mines lost money. Germany, on the other hand, did not subsidize Veba's and Saltzgitter's mines, yet they produced coal at a profit. Nora called for five steps to enable these businesses to adapt to new competitive situations:

a. closing the least productive coal mines of CDF;
b. reviewing whether this and other single-supplier monopolies should continue;
c. regrouping activities among the state monopolies and other state enterprises;
d. establishing harmony between state firms and private French firms;
e. encouraging state monopolies to meet the tests of market competition by investing overseas or by taking on foreign joint-venture partners in domestic mining operations.

2. French single-supplier monopolies need to be completely reorganized and restructured.

This recommendation prompted the government to merge Mines Domaniales de Potasse d'Alsace and Office nationale industriel de l'azote into Entreprise Minière et Chimique

(EMC, Mining and Chemical Corporation).[8] However, the placebo of organization rather than real managerial reform was not what Nora had in mind. The government created a new unified conglomerate which lacked coordination at the top and the ability to work together throughout the management and employee ranks. The potash miners of Alsace were as traditional in their work habits as the coal miners of CDF, and they refused suggestions to cut their numbers, improve their work habits, and become more productive.[9] French potash soon became overpriced and could not compete with American potash.

The two former state entities did not mesh properly because the Alsace miners were traditionalists and the chemists of the Office national industriel de l'azote were dynamic and interested in producing new compounds for the world fertilizer market. Even with a monopoly over domestic potash production and a guarantee of 25 percent of the French fertilizer market, EMC lost about $25 million in 1969—one year after becoming a single-supplier monopoly. Similar losses followed in later years.

Cosmetic changes—*regroupments* (regroupings)—were not enough. Enterprises had to have new managers, get out of unprofitable lines of business, close mines, and lay off workers.

3. These single-supplier monopolies are unable to adapt themselves to new competitive situations unless their government subsidies are reduced.

This recommendation showed an acute awareness of how France had fallen behind Germany and Holland in building up a strong base for industrial state enterprise capitalism. Unquestionably it expressed Western European feelings about the excesses of industrial state capitalism.

The French government decided to force its state monopolies to change. Neither de Gaulle's 1959 statement that "we will never renounce our coal" nor Yvon Morandat's 1968 statement as president of Houillères du Nord et du Pas de Calais (Coal Mines of the North and Pas de Calais) that "miners are always the first victims" could stop the government from merging all coal mines into CDF and to force the new state enterprise to enter the chemical business.[10]

In three years, CDF reduced its dependence on coal by 25 percent, yet still lost about $4 million in 1971. Unlike the Dutch, Germans, Norwegians, and Swedes, the French had not allowed their state enterprise managers to establish miners' wages and working conditions or to set coal prices. It thought that diversification would support all of CDF's business so that government would not have to force it to close facilities and lay off politically-sensitive workers.[11]

4. Even with CDF's coal business down to 50 percent of total sales and with the imported French-owned coal from its West Virginia mines,[12] it was clear by 1976 why state monopolies could not adapt: their governments believed they had the inherent right to intervene to the long-run detriment of these business entities.

The French government had decided once again to open new French mines and hire additional coal miners—to pursue socio-political goals in the face of cold managerial logic.[13] Aware of how costly such governmental restrictions could be, international private bankers required the French government to unconditionally guarantee the $30 million in notes offered by CDF.

Cosmetic *regroupment* will not change the views of independent bankers. Structural change without the loosening of government fetters does not promote managerial independence. The French have yet to apply to mineral monopolies the model of commercial autonomy so successful in their petroleum and petrochemical industries.

Britain Pays $18 Billion to Keep Monopolies Afloat

While the French stumbled along with CDF and EMC, the British ignored French mistakes and steadfastly maintained public ownership of "the commanding heights of the economy"—coal, steel, electricity, gas, railways, and airlines. The presumption to subsidize these single-supplier monopolies no matter what the cost remains even today.

Britain's National Coal Board was not permitted to mix state subsidies for coal production with the capital it raised for its computer sector, North Sea petroleum and gas fields, and caprolactam plant.[14] With no opportunity to reduce its commitment in coal in order to improve investments, misfortune became catastrophe in 1974, when its joint-venture caprolactam plant in Flixborough burned. That dashed hopes of the National Coal Board and DSM to offer British firms an alternative source for their nylon.[15]

Single-supplier monopolies began to claim some freedom to invest outside their industries. Indeed, the National Coal Board did exercise discretionary investment with government approval. Two years later the government ordered the Board to give up its North Sea petroleum and gas interests to the newly-formed British National Oil Corporation.[16] In conferring discretion for a time, though, government implied that a state enterprise is entitled to make new investments outside the monopolized industry in certain circumstances.

The developing single-supplier monopoly claim to commercial autonomy in investment had received a rebuff in 1975, when Britain's Labour government deferred closing British Steel's East Moors mill, agreed to close Ebbw Vale mill in South Wales, creating 3,300 labor redundancies, and decided to build a new electric-arc mill near Stoke-on-Trent, where 1,700 were to be laid off.[17] British Steel Corporation seized the occasion to insist that the government permit it to reduce its 120,000 employees to the 85,000 level of the Japanese steel industry, which produces the same amount of steel yearly. Furthermore, it said, all its obsolete and inefficient plants should be closed. Although British Steel massed the strongest arguments so far for freedom to modernize, it did not demand unchecked freedom to invest and divest.

In the 1970s, the European single-supplier state monopolies wanted more independence, secured their limited freedom of action at home, and enlarged their responsibilities for furthering national interests abroad. But governments alone still had the final say in authorizing investments and divestments, particularly when workers would be laid off. What has been the net result? Rather than allow factories to close, governments sacrifice economic growth. They refuse to let state monopolies take the usual business actions to protect their investments, turn their losses around, and make themselves competitive against imported products and in overseas markets.

Those failures come as a surprise to many. Until the

1970s, these businesses were essentially domestic. From 1945 to 1973 the spreading use of taxes to subsidize inefficient state monopolies gave their managers license to create the controlled sector of the economy they believed correct. Their decisions shrank profits, reduced investment, and slowed economic growth.[18]

No doubt nationalization and state monopolies have cost the taxpayers dearly. For Britain $18 billion in taxes have been used to cover deficits of the National Coal Board, British Steel, British Gas, and others. Except for the six-year period 1963–68, when Britain's nationalized industries did make money, Britain has ignored profits for the sake of social objectives.[19] Both Conservative and Labour governments held down prices to fight inflation while costs of all products and services bought by British monopolies rose. These governments approved of poor productivity, meddled in management, and provided only short-term or long-term loans —no medium-term loans. As Ball says, such measures shrink the most basic responsibility of ownership—the assumption of entrepreneurial risk.[20]

Throughout the postwar period, Britain refused to force monopolies to generate their own capital or go bankrupt. The government said instead that no big firms—state-owned or privately-owned—could fail. Thus the Conservatives took over ailing Rolls Royce and Upper Clyde Shipbuilders and invaded industries never before considered "the commanding heights of the economy."

Meanwhile, similar types of loss-ridden firms were being bailed out by government ownership in Italy, by direct subsidies in France and Germany, and by government-backed loans in the United States. Ironically, European conservatives and social democrats did not have the backing of national communist parties, which condemned such takeovers as "socializing losses."

Need for Competitive State Enterprises

Clearly, industrial state enterprise capitalism needs the market economy. Without it, neither workers' control in Yugoslavian factories nor the more centralized decision making prevalent elsewhere will promote entrepreneurial risk taking, allocation by competitive pricing mechanisms, or self-generation of investment capital.

Industrial state enterprise capitalism turns failures into profits not by restricting competition. Rather, it rejects the excesses of single-supplier monopolies in favor of other choices: nonmonopoly government initiatives, mixed or joint ventures, government-subsidized investments, and private decisions. This is the challenge of industrial state enterprise capitalism in the last quarter of the twentieth century.

4

Three Myths

MOST GOVERNMENTS introduced industrial enterprise capitalism into the market economy believing there were no limits to what such enterprises could accomplish. And many were chastened by their experience. After every intervention, there was a desire to swear off until business, labor, and the public demanded that governments take over ailing firms, force industrial rationalization, and promote economic development in depressed regions. Intervention always changes the structure of a market economy. What was clever and appropriate during one period becomes foolish and inappropriate in another.

Intervention is a major priority. Only with very substantial intervention can economic development be promoted, industrialization take place, and industries be rationalized. However, such interventions may not accomplish what government, business, labor, and the public believe they achieve. In fact, they may reinforce the status quo rather than offer new forms of competition and give aid rather than counter the American business challenge.

The myths about why governments intervene in their market economies are insidious. For instance, Third World countries are intervening more and more, believing that total government control over industry is best. They think that Europe met the American-backed international business challenge solely by direct and forceful government intervention. Yet the truth is that governments need to know when and how to intervene.

Intervention that promotes increased productivity and generates investment capital is appropriate. That which encourages worker inefficiencies and a poorer allocation of resources is inappropriate. Up to a point, the latter will support the former by adding to the volume of investment.[1] Beyond that point, intervention becomes a burden; it must be redirected, changed, or altered or it will crowd out productive investment. But while the rules are simple, few governments know them, and even fewer care to apply them.

Single-supplier monopolies and other state industries which are in or straddle the controlled sector of the economy have produced unimpressive results. They are increasingly facing stronger competition and need to redirect their energies, improve management of their resources and personnel, and take on new venture risks. Intervention actually lowers the potential business performance of state enterprises unless it results in increased productivity of its labor and capital measured against specific business and social gains. Otherwise, intervention is almost certain to mean a diffusion of efforts where myth replaces fact.

There are three major myths about intervention.

The first is that by investing their capital in depressed regions, state enterprises can improve regional income. But state enterprise capitalism cannot provide an instant cure for the backwardness of Britain's Wales, Sweden's Norbottens Lan, and Italy's Mezzogiorno.

The Italian experiment should once and for all explode this myth. In 1957, the Italian government set up the Fund for the South for its depressed Mezzogiorno with direct investments by state enterprises. It expected these huge investments (40 percent of their total investment) to close the income gap between north and south.[2]

The Italian state enterprises have become the principal competitors of privately-owned firms throughout Italy. The government-owned firms control more of the Italian economy than the government anticipated—300 operating companies;[3] 25 percent of the stock issued by all Italian companies;[4] and 13 percent of all bank deposits[5]—their accumulated debts. They employ 3 percent of the Italian work force and are responsible for 6.3 percent of Italy's gross fixed capital formation.[6] Yet the income gap between north and south has widened.[7]

Those in other countries who propose today that we use state enterprises to promote regional economic development are even more sanguine than the Italians were. Such schemes will have just as little impact on the prospect of regional economic development as Italian investment has had upon the Mezzogiorno. This is true in the Amazon and northeastern Brazil or Sumatra and western Java.

The implementation of industrial state enterprise capitalism without a simultaneous change in cultural perceptions, family loyalties, and work relationships has never had more than transitory impact. Regardless of how lush the inducements may be, foreign and local private businesses know better than to invest heavily. They know, for instance, that the cost of making products in Sicily and marketing them in Milan is generally 15 percent more than producing the same products in Turin, Milan, or Florence.[8]

Even with large amounts of subsidies, southern-made products tend to be noncompetitive in northern markets. There is an exception: when these products are made by subsidiaries of the state enterprise. They must buy their semifinished steel tubing and basic petroleum building-blocks as part of their overall commitment to the economic development of the Mezzogiorno. This is intrafirm transfer pricing—the way the government and industry subsidize state enterprises to maintain them over the long run.

However, intrafirm transfer pricing within Italian state enterprises is a matter of the controlled sector, not the market sector. For instance, the corporate headquarters of IRI doesn't permit its many subsidiaries to compete among themselves. Instead of promoting their growth as independent profit centers, these firms have been assigned the primary social objective of creating jobs and income within Italy's depressed south.

The legendary intervention of IRI, ENI, Montedison, and others in the Mezzogiorno rests largely on the willingness of government to subsidize their construction of "cathedrals in the desert." Every one of these investments is capital-intensive, employs some labor in make-work tasks, and operates substantially under capacity.

These lessons have not been learned throughout the Mediterranean, in Latin America, and in Southeast Asia because of the almost universal obsession with the possibilities of macroeconomic intervention. However, direct investments by state enterprises are clearly a micro business activity made up of many specific decisions at all levels of management. These include the number of possible work turns, availability of loanable funds, noninterruptible sources of power, proper transportation, and timely receipt of packaging materials. They flow against the economists' conventional wisdom and their macro view of development. Many countries are copying the Italian model without paying attention to the critical micro business issues.

The second myth is that by investing their funds in capital-intensive industries, state enterprises can transform their less-developed regions—like Sumatra and the Amazon basin—into developed regions.

Some Third World countries, like some poets and politicians, are singled out for fame far beyond the common lot, and Brazil is such a country. Like England in the nineteenth century and the United States in the twentieth century, Brazil is seen today as the less-developed country that made it—in the twenty-first century. For a decade, whenever Latin Americans, Asians and Africans have doubted their chances to compete worldwide, they have asked, "How is Brazil doing it?"

Much of the discussion concerns Petrobrás and Vale do Rio Doce. Brazilian industrialization, the popular story goes, has grown mainly from strategic government intervention through state enterprises. This explanation, which blesses the government, is attractive in Brazil. But it is false.

Macroeconomic and microeconomic phenomena are interdependent. Money supply is linked to available capital and investment in educational support for merit services provides a supply of trained employees. Important as state enterprise is to Brazilians, it is not the only cause of the miracle in Minas Gerais, São Paulo, and Brazil's other southern states, nor is it the only factor creating industrial jobs in Brazil's northeast.

As a state enterprise, Petrobrás has always been the peculiar property of Brazil's nationalists.[9] Founded under the Vargas dictatorship in 1954, when they cried "The petroleum is ours!," Petrobrás prospered and suffered respectively under the turbulent days of Kubitschek's democracy and Goulart's radicalism. It came into its own once again after the 1964 military revolution, when it was forced to compete against private interests in the petrochemical industry and in the retail distribution of gasoline.

In many ways, this close tie to the shifting fortunes of government is unfortunate. If this potential multinational could have generated internal revenues, if it had given up its belief that its sole purpose was to find oil within Brazil, and if it had eliminated speculative wildcatting, Petrobrás could have become internationally important sooner.

In 1970, the nationalists were beaten with their own old-fashioned ideas. Because Petrobrás could explore for oil only within Brazil, whether Petrobrás found oil or not it had to sink more and more wells. It had created its own market share in Brazil, some 20 percent of the retail market. But alert to their opportunities as Brazil began to thirst for oil, Petrobrás managers got permission to explore for oil in Iran, Iraq, and Madagascar and to perform other business activities which the "Seven Sisters" and petroleum state multinationals engage in.[10] These managers had formed an independent economic power base in a way that expanded their own power and wealth through their success as top management of state enterprises.[11]

While Brazil drastically restricted private, foreign, and domestic petroleum firms, Petrobrás built its own refinery capacity and captured one-fifth of the Brazilian retail gasoline market. The prototype state enterprise for Petrobrás, Vale do Rio Doce, developed its own mining and smelting operations in the 1950s and 1960s, becoming the world's largest exporter of iron ore in the 1970s.[12] Well-built, capital-intensive steel furnaces, rolling mills, and sheet metal plants rose away from Brazil's traditional southern industrial base, while farther into the Northeast was the worst unemployment and human misery outside of Bombay.

Without employable labor, skillful entrepreneurs, productive domestic research and organizations, and well-managed financial markets, state enterprises have had little impact. There is no easy solution to bringing about industrialization. Capital-intensive investments will not necessarily transform Third World economies into First World, developed economies. No matter how carefully the government restricts competition, the lack of competition allows obsolete plants to accumulate. Their products sell only in highly-protected domestic markets. The new technologies for offshore drilling or for new synthetic oil products keep the older technologies out of foreign markets and reduce their life span in protected markets as well.

Foreign and domestic manufacturers are forced to buy these outmoded products to maintain access to local capital and customer markets. Like the Italian intrafirm transfer prices, these directed purchases between Petrobrás and Vale do Rio Doce and other firms force production out of the market sector and into the controlled sector. These firms assist Brazilian industrialization because government subsidizes entrepreneurial risks. Each of their ventures requires the capital investment which private and foreign interests are unwilling to make within imposed guidelines and conditions.

These include, for example, the mining of iron ore, steel mill construction, and the mining of bauxite. Some of these

71

new ventures—for example, offshore oil drilling—require world-scale technology that Petrobrás can't supply. Therefore government must modify its control of direct investments with "risk" bidding and other measures. The government considers these investments so strategically important that it is unwilling to give private and foreign firms complete license for fear of losing control.

State enterprise investments, made up of many specific decisions at all managerial levels, are a micro business activity. Matters like choosing among competing technologies, selecting joint-venture partners, and using a management service contract determine whether state enterprises generate their own investment capital, produce improved technologies, and create productive labor forces; these are the essentials of industrialization.

It is the management of the potential multinationals that improves a nation's international position. The eight state multinational enterprises have shown the way, and National Iranian Oil is now attempting to join them.[13] The state enterprise managers of the other OPEC single-supplier monopolies can do the same.

A third myth is that by investing capital funds to reorganize industries, state enterprises will make them competitive domestically and abroad—the quick way to turn national firms into multinationals.

In the developed countries, intervention hushes its nationalistic rhetoric in favor of reasoned arguments for forced mergers, rationalized industries, and orderly marketing agreements. Governments—Conservative or Labour, Gaullist or Socialist, Christian Democratic or Social Democratic—then withdraw monopoly privileges and tell state enterprises to join with private firms to help national industries compete against America. This is how the French in particular tried to force single-supplier monopolies and other enterprises to become competitive.

This was the way CFP, Elf-Aquitaine, CDF, EMC, Renault, and others were thrust more fully into the market sector. We know why France became so restive. In the wake of German successes, both French government and business thought that France must rationalize industries with the best chance of dominating the European market. The government would also have to resist the American challenge in the 1960s. So the French consolidated five petroleum state businesses into the Elf-Erap Group in 1963, then regrouped the petrochemical interests of CFP, Elf, and others in the late 1960s and finally merged Aquitaine into the Elf Group in 1976. The government expected the Elf Group and CFP to dominate refining and marketing within the European Common Market.[14]

Indeed, these enterprises compete well against German and American firms in France and elsewhere in Europe. But they haven't dominated. Germany's Veba and its newly acquired subsidiary, Gelsenberg, form a potential multinational with new duties. Both Norway's Norsk Hydro and Statoil and Britain's BP and BNOC are trying to reduce French control over North Sea oil exploration and marketing.

Careful as the national government is in joining its domestic firms, it forces them to choose which factories, products, distribution systems, and services they will give up. None has priced these swaps out in the market to see whether they are indeed competitive. Arms-length exchanges are hard to insure under pressures of good citizenship. Some firms do well; others fare poorly. Market resistance is in the cards. Even with the best of government intentions, these firms can't compete with firms that use the open market to expand.

A variation on this theme is the forced merger—another form of government subsidy.

For instance, the regrouping of automobile and truck capacity between Renault and Peugeot didn't take place in the open market. The creation of Elf and the later merger with Aquitaine were aimed at a social goal—to build up French industry and keep Germans and Americans out.

The lesson is basic: the real work of state enterprises is not to conduct the government's macroeconomic policy; rather, it is to build new plants or acquire commercial activities which help create more jobs, additional investments, and an expanded tax base. Governments should expect industrial state enterprises to be successful on their own. Forced mergers work only when managers can cure the problems of asymmetrical financial, production, marketing, and administrative operations among dissimilar subsidiaries.

5

Missed Opportunities

STATE ENTERPRISES emerged at the same time that America became the world's foremost foreign direct investor. State subsidized enterprises using intrafirm transfer pricing schemes, directed purchasing orders, and forced conglomerate mergers didn't learn how to compete. This is why the net income share of state enterprises (Table A–2 in Appendix) remained constant but declined between 1958 and 1971.

In the 1950s, most European governments refused to close mines and factories and lay off workers, but by 1960 the Dutch government had used European Coal and Steel Community retraining funds to move DSM into new business activities. Other governments missed this opportunity; French and Italian mining firms are still far from becoming what DSM is now: a $3 billion multinational.

In 1966, France discovered that its mineral resources state enterprises had been stagnant internationally. Since establishing CDF in 1968, following publication of the Nora

Report, the French fever to make up for lost time has rivaled their drive to rationalize petroleum in the 1960s. Since they did not give CDF commercial autonomy to close mines, lay off miners, and set coal prices nor provide EMC with the same managerial responsibilities, the French mineral resources firms continued to fall behind equivalent firms elsewhere. The mineral resources firms and their chemical subsidiaries were the second-fastest growing group of state enterprises from 1971 to 1976 (Table A–3 in Appendix). This group includes the following coal, iron and steel, copper, and aluminum state enterprises:

1. Important internationals: Iscor of South Africa, Italsider, Saarbergwerke, Salzgitter, and Viag of Germany;
2. Other single-supplier monopolies: British Steel, National Coal Board of Britain, Charbonnages de France, Vöest-Alpine of Austria, and Zimco of Zambia.
3. Domestic state enterprises: Steel Authority of India.

In 1976 several other state enterprises joined this group —Brazil's Vale do Rio Doce being the most prominent. This potential state multinational now has two groups of foreign allies to speed the development of two major industries, iron and steel and bauxite and aluminum. The first group is U.S. Steel, Nippon Steel, Kobe Steel, and Italsider; the second is Norsk Hydro, Spain's Instituto Nacional de Industria, Alcan, Rio Tinto Zinc, and Reynolds Metals.[1]

French state enterprises had forfeited their right to join the multinational consortia of state- and privately-owned firms that now link emerging Third World countries with the developed world. CDF and EMC are excluded today because they didn't compete yesterday. No other state enterprise will help them. They must help themselves or fall by the wayside.

In 1976, the French followed the remedy of protecting domestic mines and factories from the ravages of the market. This improved sales of domestic state enterprises, but it did not improve profits, productivity, ability to generate capital internally, or investment strength abroad. If outsiders were let into domestic markets, the state enterprise would have to compete. The French could then develop state multinationals from firms whose top management can execute the appropriate business strategies.

The belief that the state enterprise cannot survive in open domestic markets is false. Domestic market competition does not solve long-standing managerial problems, but by refusing to force state-subsidized enterprises to change, governments only postpone their problems. To prevent repeated failures, governments must expel state enterprises from the controlled sector. Any intermediate solution can only reinforce their past mistakes.

The trade-off between opportunities to increase the performance of state enterprises and the need to control them is the single most important decision governments make—whether, when, and how to intervene. There is no easy answer or clean solution to balancing economic performance against political control. The real question is whether governments are willing to take necessary entrepreneurial risks, for business enterprises—privately-owned or state-owned—are after all creatures of the state and must conform to the nation's view of what is right and proper for society.

6

Two Intervention Strategies

MANY state enterprises have become the international business community's new challengers. They didn't succeed without struggle, however, for they sacrificed their privileged status. Governments had to decide how much managerial autonomy to grant them. Their cumulative decisions have led to the introduction of nexus relationships between government and business as a new form of international commercial power, on the one hand, desirous of building up the world-wide market position of state enterprises and, on the other hand, impelled to secure resources for nation-states.

For the majority of governments, state enterprises are rapidly becoming a competitive force in the market sector. Their sales and asset positions, as shown by their compound annual growth rates for the twenty-year period 1957–76 and for the most recent period 1971–76 (Table A–4 in Appendix), are faster than similar privately-owned, non-American business firms. At the same time, private firms are turning to their governments for more protection, more aid, and more security under the wings of state enterprises. Further struggles will take place, arising, for example from Canada's commitment to end American domination of local industries. There are fundamental struggles over economic organization—for example, in France over the number and size of computer, health care and pharmaceutical, and airframe firms, and whether government should own some or all of them, or whether government should subsidize them without having an ownership role. There are struggles over the legitimacy of government control itself in West Germany.

Two intervention strategies have been used to transform ineffective state-owned entities into competitive business firms: setting up orderly marketing agreements; and cutting apron strings, dependencies of state enterprises on home governments. Both are the work of government officials to forge appropriate linkages between government and business.

Orderly Marketing Agreements

The division of responsibility between the planning bureaucracy and the state enterprise management differs from country to country. Some governments assign their ministries more powers over prices and market supply than others do. In exchange, the state enterprises receive protected domestic markets and claims for government support, subsidy, and sustenance when things get too difficult overseas.

The English term "orderly market" does not convey what

is meant by the French term *marché ordonné* and the German term *geordneten Markt*.

Marché ordonné means state enterprise conformity to national economic plans. CFP is "A Servant of the State," "A Tool of National Oil Policy," as the *Financial Times* labels it, and as the *New York Times* calls it, "A Bulwark of Nation's Policies."[1] The French state enterprises do not depend solely on the market for success; they have a claim on the government. We ought to remember this before we agree that they should be given all the privileges of private firms when they invest in the United States or compete against American firms in third-country markets.

Americans who read foreign business periodicals already know what France is up to. As far back as 1969, Michel Drancourt wrote in *Entreprise*, the French equivalent to *Business Week*, that state enterprise was, in effect, a new form of war.[2] He said that France and other continental powers will counter the American multinational challenge by infusing industrial state enterprise capitalism with the competitive strategies of the market. To conduct this battle, the French have provided university-trained personnel—*les cadres*—in great numbers for middle-management positions in their state and private enterprises. These became immediate allies of their government mentors, a reservoir of potential government talent, and protectors of the French state capitalist system. No matter what happens to individual state enterprises or private firms, the careers of *les cadres* will progress as they move back and forth between enterprise and government.

Les cadres will help firms in trouble, help new firms prosper, rationalize industries, and seize control of high-technology industries from foreigners. They are determined to return French ownership to computers, nuclear power, and telecommunications. Most recently, the French government has "persuaded" Honeywell to reduce its holding in a French subsidiary to 45 percent and merge it with Cie. internationale pour l'informatique, and it "cajoled" ITT and Sweden's L.M. Ericsson to sell a controlling interest in their French telephone equipment companies to France's Thomson-Brandt.[3] Two new government-supported privately-owned firms have taken up their position among the "Fortune 500."

At the very least, we can expect more of this in other industries, applied in ways similar to what was done in the petroleum industry. For instance, Michel d'Ornano, the Minister of Industry and Commerce, explained why the two state enterprises, CFP and Elf-Aquitaine, should receive 80 percent of the government's tax rebate on gasoline and light oils when by law they control only half the French market. He put it bluntly: "French tax laws are intended to favor French companies."[4]

These tax concessions can be supplied with impunity as long as they are applied only against non-European Economic Community companies—that is, American firms. Article 37 of the Treaty of Rome, the rulings of the European Commission on July 24, 1963, and subsequent interpretations by many European legal scholars[5] encourage the view that French companies cannot be protected to the detriment of other European companies. Indeed, Seita, the cigarette monopoly, has been forced to compete in France itself, and some government protection over coal and potash has been removed. Nevertheless, the petroleum industry remains the preserve of *les cadres*, who continue to protect it. Petroleum state enterprise managers have been given full responsibility to develop a strategy. No other group of French state enterprise managers has gained such freedom. The government thinks that petroleum enterprises above all can be counted on to conform to the needs of the French state.

Geordneten Markt means state enterprises are surrounded by a web of influence coming from the German federal government, local governments, and their big banks.[6] In the mid 1970s, state enterprise ownership over German industry, particularly the petroleum industry, is being built into relationships with other countries in the European Common Market, in eastern Europe, and in the Third World.

There are three reasons for their activities: (1) meeting the American challenge worldwide; (2) developing a continental solution to oversupply in petrochemicals and steel; and (3) insuring German access to an adequate supply of petroleum and other vital mineral resources.

Industrial statism—defined in the recent merger case of Veba and Gelsenberg—is the notion that Germany should have one large petroleum state enterprise to compete with the "Seven Sisters" and state multinationals. The preference for orderly state-to-state marketing agreements overturns all arguments for letting forces flow independently to their own national level. It has become an axiom of European government leaders that free market forces must be subject to the economic interests of the state.

The best illustration of the arrangement by which government dictates, supports, and pushes a market policy is the German federal government's long-term insistence that Volkswagenwerk must invest directly in the United States. It is easy to criticize the German union's resistance, but the union, as well as the government of Lower Saxony, feared that domestic automobile factories would close. Since the federal government owns only 20 percent of Volkswagenwerk, a solution took years to bring about. By then VW had lost over half of its American market. This case showed unity between government and state enterprise corporate strategic purposes.

As a general rule, of course, government dictates and state enterprise obeys. The result is a set of orderly marketing agreements which can lead to the grim failures of Britain, the "cathedrals in the desert" of Italy, or the more competitive state enterprises of France and Germany. These arrangements still reflect the realities of fifteen years ago, when the intention was to protect nation-states from the American challenge.

In the early 1960s, orderly marketing agreements began to replace outright subsidies to single-supplier monopolies. Only six state enterprises then appeared in "The Fortune 100." By 1963, when "The Fortune Directory" expanded to 200 firms, nineteen state enterprises appeared; by 1971, twenty-one were listed. The thirteen that remained from the 1960s through 1971 were mainly British, French, and Italian petroleum firms and those which used European Coal and Steel Community funds to retrain coal miners and iron workers or to close mines: DSM, Italsider, National Coal Board, and Salzgitter. Other state enterprises equally subject to special orderly marketing agreements also remained on the list from 1963 to 1971: Aerospatiale (military aircraft supplier to the French government); Iscor (South Africa's main source of domestic iron and other minerals); Renault (one domestic supplier of trucks to the French government); and Volkswagenwerk.

In the early 1960s, orderly marketing agreements were designed to protect the nation-state; today they are used to compete. There is now a deliberate policy to advance state enterprises at the expense of privately-owned—mainly American—firms. Some state enterprises dropped off the *Fortune* list because even with special arrangements they couldn't maintain sufficient growth in sales. But thirteen state enterprises stayed on the list by increasing sales and asset position. Most importantly, they remained in the top 100.

Today, orderly marketing agreements are being used to enhance the commercial power of the nation-state. Japan's provision of long-term debt capital through government banks to about 100 "Fortune 500" firms is a good example of how governments have expanded the use of orderly marketing agreements to government-supported private firms. South Korea, Brazil, and Finland follow this example. With one-half of the "Fortune 500" owned and supported—in fact subsidized—by their home governments, we see the full power of the nexus at work in the international economy.

The success of these firms is due largely to their home governments providing them with special benefits, incentives, and preferences not available to typical private investors. Yet with this success has come the government's desire to force their most competitive enterprises further into the market sector.

Cutting Apron Strings

What we have in France are specific binding agreements, based on Nora's Report, between the government and outstanding state enterprises. Firms can maintain their own cash reserves (something which the French state has always jealously guarded and something which Canadian crown corporations are yet unable to do), lay off or retrain redundant workers, invest in profit-making opportunities outside their traditional markets, and enter into joint ventures with foreign firms at home or in third-country markets.

The market sector French state enterprises are free of most government fetters. They can do what they will, provided they meet basic national socio-economic needs—employment, income, resources, and markets. Renault, for instance, has no problem working within these guidelines. When it had serious labor troubles in 1971, the government did not step in. Rather, it lived up to its contract and permitted Renault to settle with its workers on its own.

Even though the French government has given Renault, CFP, Elf-Aquitaine, and others more managerial freedom than it has the two controlled-sector enterprises (CDF and EMC), we should never forget that French industrialization depends upon the government. All French state enterprises and government-supported firms rely on the state in times of fiscal difficulties, when new regional economic development priorities have been established, and during periods of extreme national peril, such as the 1973 oil boycott.[7]

The French government-business nexus is not a partnership, as the English and Americans view it. Rather, it is government tutelage over business.[8] It flows from centuries of thought which assumes government's absolute right to command the obedience of business. The relative freedom of managerial action so recently granted Renault and Elf could be suddenly and severely restricted or ended. For the 1970s, this government is encouraging its automobile and petroleum state enterprises to embrace the market sector and forswear privileges still open to other French state enterprises.

Both firms are to follow the example of CFP. In fact, Elf is now able to pay the government a shareholder's dividend. With its recent acquisition of Aquitaine, it has served notice that it will compete with CFP worldwide.

We must pay attention to the steady spread of market-oriented state enterprises designed to implement a nation's economic policies. Others in Europe, North America, and in the Third World are following the French example.

Market-sector State Enterprises

Today, the Canadian government is seeking to end the special status of its crown corporations. The time has come to give them the ability to keep their own reserves and to push them out from under the thumb of the prime minister and the government in power. If they oppose such changes, they will be forced into becoming subsidiaries of the market-sector state enterprises—government-owned, but able to keep their own reserves, negotiate their own labor contracts, and enter into joint-venture agreements with foreign firms.

A major example is Polysar, a crown corporation established during the Second World War as a wartime measure. For thirty years Polysar had reported to Parliament through the Ministry of Defence Production. In 1972, the Canada Development Corporation took over Polysar. Without crown corporation status, Polysar lost its special arrangements with Canada's defense establishment and federal government. Polysar is unusual because it built up a network of foreign direct investments in France, Belgium and the United States and continued to expand these styrene, latex, and rubber-mixing facilities in Ohio, Massachusetts, and Tennessee after becoming a subsidiary of a government-owned corporation.

Now that Polysar's new relationship is firmly established, it is possible to see how much the ending of dependency relationships liberates state enterprises. In the Canadian case, the risk of market failure—a risk Polysar had unconvincingly tried to bear—was to be absorbed not by the government itself, but by a government-owned corporation. Its function is to invest government risk capital in firms willing to accept advice and counsel and to pay dividends.

Devising and building such a corporate strategy is one of the innovations of government-business relationships in the 1970s. Other developed countries, including the United States, could do it too by giving less attention to ideology and more attention to substantive benefits.

The success of this strategy is evident in Sweden. In 1971, the government set up Statsföretag as a holding company to bring together the government's diverse dependent state enterprises. The plan was to make the profitable ones more profitable and turn loss-ridden firms into profitable ones.[9] Statsföretag was to operate on commercial lines and to pay the government a dividend within three years. Indeed, all government suggestions for new investments had to meet market tests before Statsföretag would undertake them, or the government had to agree to subsidize them for the full amount of the expected losses. Statsföretag did pay a three percent dividend. Despite great pressure from the Socialist government, Statsföretag was able to forestall its involvement in investments that did not have a market rate of return.

The rules on termination in Sweden are a bit more complicated than most, given the sharp difference of opinion between the market activities of the firm and public, socialist attitudes. Even so, these examples in France, Canada, and Sweden, together with those we've mentioned before in Brazil and Spain, show that cutting apron strings usually helps state enterprise capitalism to mature.

Capital Markets Judge Success

All emerging state enterprises can benefit from private investment capital. We do not know how much state enterprises owe international bankers. Previously, bank consortia gave firms like CDF medium-term financing only when home governments guaranteed the loans. More market-oriented firms have received such loans without guarantees. The "tombstone ads" in the world's financial press suggest that these emerging enterprises have met the tests of the market. Although the equity ownership remains in the hands of the government, this use of the world's capital markets for new investment capital is a major move on the road toward commercializing these firms.

In 1977, British National Oil Corporation went into the capital markets to raise $700 million from Citibank, Chase Manhattan, and Morgan Guaranty "to establish itself as a viable commercial operation."[10] It could have drawn on $900 million in government-guaranteed funds, but it chose not to. It preferred to disassociate itself from the state-subsidized, single-supplier monopolies and perennial money losers such as British Steel and the National Coal Board. It wants to build a reputation as a market-sector firm.

Another way to raise new venture capital—used mainly by Austria and Germany—is the actual sale of equity shares to non-government buyers: domestic and foreign bankers, industrialists, and individuals. Austria sold off five of its properties to local interests in the 1950s, but its oil and steel firms remain government-owned. Germany sold off Preussag in 1959 and 80 percent of Volkswagenwerk in 1961.

By going public, VW gained access to insurance and bank funds, enabling it to recapitalize and issue $286 million worth of stock. The American Securities and Exchange Commission cautioned Americans against buying this stock. It said that the statistical manuals in general use "contain no mention of the company or of the shares . . . and that the company's balance sheets, profit and loss statements, and earnings report are all lacking."[11] Despite this warning, Chemical Bank of New York provided American Depository Receipts within one month after the VW shares were traded in Frankfurt and Hamburg. German banks ran newspaper ads and put up point-of-purchase displays to advertise the availability of VW stock to the German public, to induce VW employees to buy the stock, and to encourage parents with three or more children to take advantage of five percent rebate on the stock.[12] The sales yielded investment capital to expand manufacturing capacity in Brazil and to make the United States a major export market. Today, VW is one of the more widely-traded state enterprise securities in the world, with access to both debt and equity capital throughout the developed countries. Very few state enterprises, save BP, enjoy such a position.

Along the same lines, but not similar to the VW denationalization, are the state enterprises which have always had private shareholders along with government shareholders. British, French, Norwegian, Italian and German profitable state enterprises confirm that market performance depends partly on confidence among private investors. Governments have had the insight to force state enterprises to work closely with world private capital markets. Governments themselves find they like the freedom to enter and exit these markets as their needs change.

Thus, the British government sells off some shares of BP while the Norwegian government buys enough shares of Norsk Hydro to gain 51 percent control over it as Norway prepares to exploit its oil bonanza. Both Italy and Germany use these same equity markets to purchase additional shares of Montedison and Veba respectively to influence new investment strategies. This short circuits the long and sometimes acrimonious debates in parliaments about whether government should rationalize the Italian textile and German petroleum industries.

Ideology versus Pragmatism

Denationalization is a problem of ideology. It is also a problem of will. The relatively small diminution in government's power to force state enterprises to do what government wants is too much to sacrifice. It resembles reprivatization, where governments return to a laissez faire posture. Yet this is one problem where ideology must be overcome, where reason must rule.

7

The Common Market Cooperates

SOME state enterprises take advantage of their new freedom of action and become leaders in expanding foreign trade. Others successfully challenge the American multinationals with foreign direct investments in Third World countries. As a result, many state enterprises, especially those freed from unnecessary restraints abroad, grew stronger because governments opened up their domestic markets. This is why the sales share of state enterprises (Table A–1 in Appendix) increased so much between 1962 and 1976, and why the compound annual rate of sales and asset growth (Table A–4 in Appendix) was far greater for state enterprises than for non-American private firms.

In the 1950s, most European governments refused to open their domestic markets to widespread competition. By the early 1960s, all six member governments of the European Economic Community accepted more trade in goods and direct capital investments. As intra-Community customs duties were phased out during the 1960s for the original six members (Germany, France, Italy, The Netherlands, Belgium, and Luxembourg) and during the 1970s for the three new members (United Kingdom, Ireland, and Denmark), Community regulations assumed local state enterprises could receive no better treatment from their home governments than privately-owned domestic firms and foreign private and state enterprises.* Tax exemptions, subsidies, and the absorption of losses were all considered unacceptable support arrangements for state enterprises and government-supported private firms when these preferential agreements worked against firms from other Community countries. Yet the French government in particular continued to provide orderly marketing agreements for its petroleum, coal, and potash state enterprises throughout the transition period.

During this period, the Community assumed that local fiscal commercial monopolies would not carry out anticompetitive behavior while trying to raise tax revenue for their national governments. In 1962, the European Commission restrained Seita from keeping other European cigarettes out of the French market.[1] In 1962, the Commission ordered the French potash monopoly to buy potash from other Common Market countries on the same basis as French potash.[2] And in 1963, the Commission declared the French petroleum system a monopoly for purposes of Article 37, which requires that state businesses adjust gradually to free

* See Articles 37 and 90 of the Treaty of Rome, and Article 44 of the Act of Accession.

market competition rather than be eliminated altogether.*
And the Community ordered France to stop subsidizing
CFP and Elf at the expense of ENI.³

Seita had a hard time adjusting to the new rules. Between
1965 and 1969, its sales rank dropped from 150 to 191 out
of the 200 largest non-American industrial firms; its actual
sales increased a mere $9 million. Because it was slipping
behind, Seita slowed the importation of European brands
to a trickle. In 1973, the Commission again cautioned
Seita.⁴

Seita had failed to take advantage of the open market.
Rather than producing "blonde" or American-type cigarettes, it insisted then, and still does, on keeping its "brown"
cigarettes—*Les Gitanes*—as its main export. *Les Gitanes*
have an image of being strong-tasting and peculiarly French,
and there is a large black market for cut-rate British and
American cigarettes.⁵

From the start of the European Common Market, Italy
agreed that its state enterprises had to compete domestically, in Europe, and in Africa. All the "Seven Sisters" and
CFP explored for oil and natural gas alongside ENI within
Italy, and many built nationwide retail marketing systems
there as well.⁶ From the late 1950s onward, ENI built up
a retail marketing system throughout Western Europe and
Africa that came to rival its nearest European competitors.⁷
Italian state enterprises joined ENI in linking northern Italy
to the other Common Market countries during the great
spurt in Italian economic growth and remain in the major

* This Commission view is widely shared by European Economic
Community legal scholars. However, some suggest that Article 37 calls for
complete elimination of state monopolies and that no new state monopolies
could be established.

world markets because they learned how to compete, first in Europe and then in Africa. They now help other state enterprises in Latin America and Asia through joint ventures, management service contracts, and engineering-consulting ventures.[8]

Will Italian state enterprises keep growing? In 1974, they were denied the best rates of interest for international loans because of the state of the Italian economy.[9] In this case, the close tie between state economic policies and the firm's commercial activities hurt IRI and ENI. When the Italian economy slumped, Italy's state enterprises suffered.

State enterprises must do their own selling job, too. They must reject the siren call of the controlled sector and insist on competing. Taking control of ailing domestic retail marketing systems when foreign firms leave, as ENI is doing, only reinforces ties to the controlled sector.

8

How State Multinationals Grew

THE EIGHT state multinational enterprises (Table A–5 in Appendix) did not arise by design. The pattern of development, which occurred sometimes randomly, sometimes purposely, generally followed six steps:

1. Government loosened its control;
2. Firms became more successful;
3. Enterprises such as coal producers became petrochemical firms—they diversified;
4. Firms used foreign technology and marketing connections;
5. Management invested in foreign markets;
6. State enterprises prospered in the international economy.

Europeans never wondered how their support and subsidy would affect entrepreneurial risk-taking and managerial performance. Governments encouraged diversifying, joining forces with foreign firms, making foreign investments, and

95

competing world-wide. Yet governments also tried to control the firms to assure vital production and keep foreign firms out of domestic markets. Since key foreign markets had commercial subsidiaries, government shareholders received decent dividends.

After two decades of give and take, governments and the eight multinationals worked out a clear relationship. Governments retained ultimate control, but clear boundaries were set mutually. How state enterprises became multinationals even with the government intervening occasionally in basic risk-taking decisions is one of the least known success stories in the world.

When the Dutch government started to turn its ailing DSM into a prosperous industrial chemical company, the enterprise had three unusual advantages.

1. It had always been a commercial company. Costs had to be covered by revenues and new investment capital had to come from retained company earnings.
2. Its small chemical division agreed to be a nucleus for an ambitious reorganization to support new research and to market promising products.
3. Its relations with unions were excellent. There had been no strikes in fifty years, and workers agreed to be retrained and relocated while helping the firm expand.

DSM was able to shut its nonproductive mines and transfer 15,000 miners to chemical plants or other industries.[1] Ten thousand retired early with pensions; 5,000 were repatriated or given other forms of compensation. Within a decade, the firm's chemical operations had built such a good technical reputation that its twenty world-wide subsidiaries and affiliates could not meet the demand for joint ventures and licensing agreements.

The government instructs this enterprise to make profits

and to raise needed capital just as other firms. The enterprise's plans to expand its product line and enter international markets has surely increased competition faced by American private firms.

Since 1968, France has hoped that CDF would follow this lead. The French firm has diversified into chemicals, reducing its dependency on coal from 90 percent in 1968 to 50 percent in 1976.[2] The chemical subsidiary, CDF-Chimie, has no technical reputation, though, and cannot expand.

Closing redundant coal mines would help, but it would not be enough. To become a state multinational, a firm must create a strategy linking technical research to marketing, financial acumen to production capacity, and new organizational templates to capabilities of top management.

Diversification

When they diversify, state multinationals participate in rationalizing industries, regrouping firms, and terminating subsidies. The strategy is to broaden product spread, increase international market penetration, and insure that all production and marketing systems contribute their share to sales, profits, improved cash flow, and investment returns.

The strategy of diversification by the eight multinationals was geared to the market sector. Governments did not push these investments for political, noncompetitive reasons. In fact, where two or more state multinationals exist in the same country—e.g., France and Italy—they compete for industries, firms, products, and markets.

In France, for example, Aquitaine understood early that

its supply of natural gas from Lacq would run out in the 1980s. To survive, it would have to find other products, markets, and systems of organization. So Aquitaine-Organico (now Aquitaine Total Organico) was organized in the mid-1960s to produce plastics, and in 1972 CFP bought a half-share of it to provide capital needed to market the newest technical discovery, the versatile plastic Rilsan.[3] Aquitaine Total Organico also combined its plastic bag subsidiary, Société Polypapier, with several German firms (Metzeler and Platte-Bonn-Mauser) to produce plastic food wrappings —"Handy Bags"—to be distributed throughout the European Economic Community.[4] If the Europeans do not do something about the high fragmentation of this industry, it will be dominated by larger American firms.

At the same time, Aquitaine Total Organico combined its paint subsidiary, La Seigneurie, with several other French paint firms to create greater economies of scale in this fragmented industry. However, the firm competes head-on with another French grouping sponsored by CDF-Chimie, Ripolin - Georget - Freitag and Helic - VanCauwenberghe, which is more than twice as large.[5]

Aquitaine Petroleum's most ambitious effort to diversify is the purchase of several French cosmetic, health care, and animal nutrition firms, or *Laboratoires*—Yves Rocher, Robillard, Labaz, Castaigne, DPSAM Vetagri, CEVA, Roger et Gallet, Parcor, Choay, and Institut Pasteur Production. The 1973 merger of all of these into a new corporate subsidiary, Sanofi, created one French state enterprise voice in the health care industry, which is strong enough to compete effectively against the Swiss, Americans, British, and Germans.[6] Three years later, Sanofi proposed to Michel d'Ornano, the Minister of Industry, a plan to join privately-owned French pharmaceutical firms in using government funds for a national health-care marketing system like that in the petroleum industry.[7] Since the French president has yet to endorse this scheme, Sanofi must continue to create its own production and marketing system without government support for an orderly marketing agreement covering the entire industry.

Micro business activities such as diversification determine whether state enterprises become multinationals. No longer can managers plead for new government policy before they can improve performance. Under industrial state multinational enterprise capitalism, diversification emerges as a major corporate strategy, but above all it is a major opportunity for state enterprise managers to show that they are as competent as private-sector managers.

ENI Breaks into World
Petroleum Markets

Some state multinationals have great reputations. ENI (Italy's National Hydrocarbon Corporation) is remembered as the petroleum firm that in the 1950s signed breakthrough agreements with the oil-producing countries, ending for all time the one-sided deals favored by the "Seven Sisters." A reference to ENI is shorthand for managerial sophistication.

For two decades, whenever Europeans, Latin Americans, Asians and Africans doubted their chances to create world-scale state enterprises, they have asked, "How is ENI doing it?"

This Italian state enterprise—contrary to legend—made

peace with Exxon, one of the "Seven Sisters," because both Enrico Mattei and Eugenio Cefis, Mattei's successor, had become friendly with William Scott, an executive vice-president of Exxon, during the "affair of the Iranian consortium."[8] After both companies withdrew their legal suits, Exxon agreed in 1963 to supply ENI with crude at a price that undercut the Russians and persuaded the other "sisters" to use ENI Genoa-to-Ingolstadt pipeline and to bring ENI into the Trans-Alpine pipeline system. In turn, ENI sold its British retail-marketing system to Exxon in 1965. From then on, the two firms worked together building refineries in Italy's depressed south, providing crude, refined products, and natural gas for Italian cars and power plants, and carrying out joint trade and investment projects. Loyalty combined with the need to buy technology and managerial experience have been the building blocks upon which ENI built itself into an $8 billion multinational.

When Italy's financial holding company, IRI, began to produce inexpensive steel in the early 1960s, it had a twofold charge: (1) to produce a good quality, inexpensive steel for Italy's private engineering and consumer-goods industries to form the export base for the Italian economic miracle; and (2) to produce as much of this steel as possible in Italy's depressed south.[9]

IRI then set up Finsider to control 70 percent of Italy's iron and steel holdings: Italsider (74 percent), Dalmine (51.2 percent), Armco (50 percent), Terni (80 percent), and Breda and Comansider (each 100 percent).[10] The remaining shares were owned by U.S. Steel, other private firms, and by Italian industrialists who used to dominate the industry. Since 1963, the combination of American and other foreign technology and Italian capital and management has been so successful that either Finsider (from 1963 to 1968) or Italsider (from 1969 to 1977) have appeared in "the Fortune Directory." Italsider's sales increased by 350 percent in seven years, while the iron and steel state enterprise has been profitable in all but one of the fourteen years it has appeared.

Montedison, a government-supported private firm until 1970, also combined with foreign private firms to enhance its product spread in domestic markets and begin to penetrate foreign markets. For example, it bought technology from and produced, in Italy, polyethylene and propylene oxide with Union Carbide, pharmaceuticals and related health-care products with Monsanto, raw materials for carpeting and upholstery with Hercules, glass with PPG and Glaverbel (Belgian), and aluminum with Alusuisse (Swiss).[11] This state enterprise, however, was not as successful as ENI or Italsider in using these foreign resources to propel itself into long-term, sustained profits.

One reason is that Montedison is itself the product of a merger in 1966 of two very dissimilar corporations—firms whose top management and employees preferred to watch each other rather than pay attention to changes in the market. In 1969, ENI and IRI bought a total of 10 percent of Montedison's stock. Since their nine out of the twenty-six members of the board of directors have veto power over all decisions, the company is a state enterprise subject to the demands of the Italian state.[12] Later share purchases by banks and state enterprises show the government owning between 25 percent and 44 percent of the firm.[13] Between 1970 and 1975, Eugenio Cefis, once the head of ENI and now chief executive officer of Montedison, maneuvered to keep the large private investors at bay (e.g., the Agnelli

family, which owns Fiat), to oust rival privately-owned textile firms from their positions of influence over Montedison,
and through state enterprise equity holdings to confirm his
control over Montedison.[14] The firm has become a third
major Italian industrial state enterprise. Its contest with
ENI demonstrates how Italian state enterprises compete
among themselves for power and influence.

Montedison and ENI (the latter through its subsidiary
ANIC [Azienda Nazionale Chimica, National Chemical
Firm]) compete in primary chemicals and in more sophisticated petrochemicals. In the future, the two will divide responsibilities: ENI will dominate refining and primary
chemicals; and Montedison (with ANIC as its subsidiary)
will dominate more sophisticated petrochemicals.[15] So far,
no Italian government has been strong enough to impose
its solution for the chemical sector. ENI would lose a profitable subsidiary and be confined to the petroleum sector.
Montedison, with ANIC, would become the dominant petrochemical firm in Italy.

Besides having to carry out their activities profitably,
Italian state enterprises must learn how to play Byzantine
politics to survive and prosper within Italy. The intensity
of the game is unique to Italy. However, it is one of the facts
of business life which every state enterprise must deal with.

Joint Ventures

State multinational capitalism requires a forward-looking,
joint-venture strategy linking research and technical sales to
the most modern technologies. It also means sharing in the

search for new sources of oil and minerals through joint exploration and production in the North Sea, in the Amazon, and elsewhere. How well industrial state enterprises do in signing themselves up with the best set of partners will determine which of the three Italian state multinationals remain international in scope and which of the emerging Brazilian, Norwegian, German, and other state enterprises become truly multinational.

The strategy of joint-venture investments followed was a matter of the market sector. By joining forces with foreign firms, state multinationals expand their business interests and penetrate domestic and foreign markets with products having gross margins. The consistent result: increased sales, assets position, and profitability.

The lesson of the Dutch, French, and Italian state enterprises is decisive. Spanish state enterprise managers did not wait for a change in government policy before going out to form joint ventures with Vale do Rio Doce, Norsk Hydro, Alcan, U.S. Steel, and Fiat. They took immediate steps to insure Spain's access to raw materials, Instituto Nacional de Industria's (National Industrial Institute) participation in most advanced mining technologies, and the chance for Spanish managers to learn how to produce and market steel, cars, and petrochemicals on a world scale.[16]

Foreign Direct Investments

Foreign direct investment is necessary in order for state enterprises to become multinationals. State enterprises must decide that their comparative advantages through new technologies, better production processes, more skillful market-ing practices, good sources of low-cost financing, better or-ganizational capabilities, and greater economies of scale outweigh the costs of competing against domestic firms at a distance through exports.

Advantages at home don't necessarily translate into simi-lar advantages abroad. Additional profits must be obtained through foreign production, although it costs less to modify products and services to match local tastes than to buy local companies. Multinationals have a special advantage in ex-pertise. They know how to put differentiated production and marketing systems in place, add new technologies, and organize and manage these systems within a complex world-wide framework. Multinationals provide nation-states with access to a widening stream of new products carefully tailored to local market tastes. They can be innovative in spreading products and can use skilled management more efficiently —no excess capacity exists among finance, marketing, per-sonnel, and planning executives.

Much of this foreign direct investment is not a substitu-tion for exports, as some have suggested. Rather, it is the result of following competitors into key markets to match one's investment rivals dollar-for-dollar in North American, European, and Third World markets. The firm with the best information system will be first to relocate production to a new, favorable national market. Its competitors, who monitor its actions, will follow because they too consider market conditions favorable.

VW in Brazil

Twenty-five years ago, VW was wholly-owned by the German federal government. It was unhampered by the need to get the Lower Saxony government and the unions to agree with their prospective corporate decisions. VW took advantage of a change in the mood of the Brazilian government, which abandoned its passive dependence on Detroit in favor of active support for the creation of an automobile industry in São Paulo.[17] This import-substitution industry would reduce strain on Brazil's balance of payments. VW's investment in Brazil was Germany's largest foreign direct investment of the 1950s.

Today, VW has $120 million of invested capital and $72 million of reinvested profits in its Brazilian facilities.[18] With an initial two-thirds share of the Brazilian market, it thought it could dominate this market indefinitely, but Ford, GM, and Fiat punctured this dream.[19] In the mid-1970s, VW is faced with a slowdown in the growth of the Brazilian market as the government seeks to stem its balance of payments drain, as the upper and middle classes worry about the high cost of gasoline and its potential shortage, and as Brazilians try a change of pace from the common Beetle.[20]

VW Paces Renault

In spite of VW's strict adherence to local content laws, both VW do Brasil and VW de México did not turn out to be import-substituting foreign direct investments.[21] In

Mexico, 70 percent of every VW had to be made from parts and assemblies made in Mexico.[22] Local car production swelled import bills and balance-of-payments deficits. In 1974, the two host governments pressured VW into a Third World-sponsored orderly marketing agreements to balance out the foreign trade in auto parts. The agreement works like this: VW do Brasil sends parts of one model to Mexico for assembly in the Puebla plant, and VW de México sends parts of a different model to Brazil for assembly in São Paulo. Each plant uses enough locally-made parts to conform to the local content laws. This complementation agreement permits each subsidiary to offer its national market an additional model otherwise impossible to build.

VW do Brasil also stepped up its export of Brazilian-made engines to its plants in Germany and to its American distribution facilities.[23] VW hoped that such exports would eventually reduce the imbalance between VW do Brasil's exports and imports. Its exports are currently one half of its Brazilian imports. VW is, as Brazilian nationalists claim, similar to all multinationals—an importer of foreign technology, an exporter of domestic profits, and a firm which should be under the control of the Brazilian nation-state.

These changes aside, VW has begun a bold new world-scale integrative corporate-planning strategy seeking to capitalize on its multinational strengths. First, it simultaneously introduced a single new model—a "world" car—called Golf in Germany, the Rabbit in the United States, and the Brasilia in Brazil.[24] Second, it is stepping up its exports of this and other models to its Common Market neighbors and EEC-affiliated Third World countries. Third, it is cutting its production losses by selling its Australian subsidiary and by not increasing its capital investment in South Africa.[25] Finally, and most importantly, it is building its own production plant in New Stanton, Pennsylvania.[26]

But Renault has successfully ousted VW from first place among European auto makers. The 1977 "Fortune Directory" placed Renault in eighth place with sales of $9.4 billion versus VW's $8.5 billion—thirteenth place. VW had waited too long.

This is Renault's strategic plan for competing against VW and others.

1. *Exports.* In 1974 Renault overtook VW in total number of cars and trucks exported to other Common Market countries, the United States, Canada, Third World countries, and to the socialist countries of Cuba and Eastern Europe.[27] Renault plans to keep its lead and to reduce VW's market share even further in southern Africa, Australasia, and North America.

2. *Production and marketing systems.* Renault provides all interested countries with a complete package of services —plant construction, design of cars, production machinery, personnel training, financial backing, and shipping services.[28] Its policy is to introduce products in as many markets as possible by providing the client country with a turnkey operation for producing cars and trucks. For instance, Renault licenses the production of its baby model, the gas-efficient R-5, in Iran, works with the Argentine government to export Renaults made in Argentina to Cuba, and operates Viennese switch houses to find outlets for goods produced in the socialist and Third World countries. These countries can thereby earn enough foreign exchange to pay for their imported Renault parts, engines, assemblies, and cars.[29]

Renault produces cars and trucks in twenty-nine different countries, using many different combinations of export and import programs, assembly facilities, full-line production overseas, international sales and marketing services, and financial arrangements to increase its volume of sales and to earn profits.

3. *The American market.* Renault differs with VW on plans for the United States. Renault sees this market as a major opportunity for exports rather than for foreign direct investments. Through its joint distribution agreement with American Motors Co., Renault obtains access to AMC's dealer and repair service network as well as adding the four-wheeled Jeep to its worldwide product-line.

4. *Diversification.* Within France and the European Economic Community, Renault views the automobile market as stagnant for at least five years. The French government views Renault as its own Institute for the Reconstruction of Industry. The government insists Renault take over ailing machine tool firms and rationalize the industry under Reit, its wholly-owned subsidiary, which seeks to export at least 50 percent of its production.[30] Renault has also agreed to rationalize the French motorcycle and truck industries.

5. *The French government link.* Renault is apparently willing to participate in rationalizing, regrouping, and diversifying those industries which the government wants to be its leading exporters of French technology, goods, services, capital, and culture.

Besides the international business strategies discussed above, the government permits a host of alternative arrangements to enhance the French industrial position worldwide. For example, French firms can organize a *Groupement d'intérêts économique* (Economic Interest Group, GIE).

This export-investment organization provides for joint research into markets, joint purchasing of parts, components and assemblies, and for joint distribution of products overseas. The French government charges no taxes on the business generated by the GIE, so French firms can undercut American firms in Third World markets. Renault and other French firms are using this strategy to test and break into new markets before committing large amounts of French capital and French prestige.

How State and Private
Multinationals Differ

By using cross-border investments among their home countries to invest in developed and Third World countries, state multinationals act like privately-owned multinationals. But there is a special twist: state multinationals follow the specific trade and investment objects of their home governments as they plan corporate strategy. The success of industrial state multinational enterprise capitalism rests on how well the eight state multinationals and the other ambitious state enterprises integrate national and corporate objectives into a unified strategy. The number of state enterprises on the verge of becoming multinationals has grown so rapidly that we must understand their role in the international economy. We must pay attention also to the growing number of private firms which are receiving injections of government equity capital so that they can link themselves more closely to American capital, technology, and marketing systems (Poclain to J. I. Case, Pechiney and Mitsui to AMAX, Fujitsu to Microtechnology Corporation): all done at the behest of foreign governments. The stimulating nation-state mix—the nexus—appears to be stronger than the sum of its parts, a totally new and formidable force in the international economy.

PART THREE

The Nexus:
A Partnership
That Works

9

Commercial Autonomy

BY DISTRIBUTING POWER between government and enterprise in a consistent and mutually acceptable fashion, the nexus changes what is meant by business performance. Good results mean friendly relations with former colonies and are measured in terms of command over resources, markets, and trade routes. Performance is both the ability to obtain a larger share of vital resources and the ability to support home governments in time of national peril. Results do *not* necessarily mean profits and higher yields on invested capital, important as these goals are. The first test of a state enterprise and the fundamental requirement for its survival is loyalty to its home government. And profits are not, by definition, essential to meeting this goal.

Compatible Goals

These relationships must be mutually acceptable: the goals of society, the state enterprise, and the people who administer government and manage the firm must be consistent. How do home country goals become the goals of the enterprise and ultimately of its management?

Since industrial state enterprises are primarily concerned with manufacturing and marketing goods, their activities must further local employment, regional income, and national balance-of-payments objectives of the home government as traditional export expansion programs have done. To achieve these purposes it is important that enterprises carry out activities with foreign-based resources and within foreign markets. The newer foreign direct investment programs of state enterprises and government-supported private firms are seeking to accomplish these tasks too.

The first concern of state enterprise management is to make the nexus operate in favor of the enterprise; therefore, it must minimize the risks of any development that threatens its commercial autonomy.

For instance, a change in government which brings the socialist left to power is a clear danger to the enterprise, but sometimes it can't be prevented. Therefore, no matter how internationally important a state enterprise is or how carefully it has weighed its domestic and foreign responsibilities, an election can throw its best-laid plans awry. It is a tribute to state enterprise management that such a destructive shift in the home government-state enterprise nexus has been held to a minimum.

Such shifts can occur with a vengeance where national

governments are supported by militant unions. These governments are required to exercise their control over "the commanding heights of the economy." In the post-Second World War period, British Steel Corporation was nationalized, denationalized, and nationalized once again.[1] Now that the ownership question is settled the fight over power within the nexus is about which mills to keep open or to close, how many mill-hands to lay off, where new mills should be built, what role the enterprise should play in the European steel cartel, and what investments British Steel should make overseas to guarantee supplies of foreign iron ore.[2]

When BP had to give up valuable North Sea properties to the government's British National Oil Corporation,[3] BP's Sir Eric Drake and his successor, David E. C. Steel, bitterly complained about the new terms for their continued access to Britain's new source of domestic oil. Why should the government place its faith in a new petroleum enterprise rather than its own member of the "Seven Sisters?" The answer lies in home government policy: to create a domestic petroleum industry, from exploration, lifting, transportation, refining, to marketing, that ends Britain's large balance-of-payments deficits.[4] Unlike Arabian and Alaskan oil, North Sea oil is available to Britain at the cost of lifting from the floor of the sea. No OPEC price schedule or the value added in refining and transporting—all raising the foreign exchange price of imported oil—need be included in calculating the costs of oil delivered to the United Kingdom from its own North Sea source. These funds could be used for investments in the Welsh and Scottish economies. No such luxury was available to Britain before.

It is this pressure of domestic economic policies that has

caused the British government to reassert its long-dormant powers over BP. No single ideological battle between Labour and BP's management would have led government to do what it is doing. In fact, domestic British policy may soon spill over into what BP does with its Alaskan oil profits. Repatriated American dividends are to be used to build up North Sea fields to reduce Britain's foreign exchange burden even further.[5]

Long-term Stability

Once established, power relationships favoring home governments tend to be stable. This shows that commercial autonomy is granted with the clear understanding that new organizations, strategies, and work assignments be established to accomplish goals favorable to the home country.

Stability is partly protection against the American-owned multinational, which can quickly wipe out years of state enterprise work with new technological and marketing techniques. State enterprises know that since they haven't been as profitable as their privately-owned counterparts, they have less access to new funds necessary to compete well.

The pattern of stability is far more important than the precise division of responsibility. In the 1920s, 1960s, and 1970s, France intervened to set up new organizations for its petroleum industry. It guaranteed them a secure domestic market, reasonable prices for their crude, and freedom to explore for oil in Iraq, Algeria, Gabon, Canada, and the United States. Neither CFP nor Elf-Aquitaine could have operated successfully without government capitalization and supporting foreign economic policy objectives.

The relationships reveal a government's commitment to alternative goals. It can confine a state enterprise to the home market; it can make it international in order to get better access to foreign raw materials; or it can turn it into a multinational. A government may have to compromise between investing at home and permitting expansion abroad. Governments hard-pressed by domestic economic difficulties—such as Britain and Italy—are likely to press for more investment at home to the detriment of their state enterprises. Still, Brazil's economic difficulties are equally great, yet its wants its enterprises to invest overseas if for no other reason than to find oil and coal for home use.

Power relationships within the nexus will not necessarily be the same from country to country. Nor can we assume that a home government's goals and those of their state enterprises and government-supported private firms—much less the intensity of the commitment to these goals—will be the same in any two cases.

A Public Policy for the 1980s

Partners in the nexus have to understand their responsibilities. Government must clearly define how much it will intervene in the industrial market sector; state enterprises must know just how autonomous they are; and government-supported privately-owned firms must learn where they fit in the rationalization and foreign market penetration programs of their home governments. All of this serves admirably the two most important goals of the nexus: economic growth at home and economic power abroad.

The division of responsibility within the nexus is a critical public policy for the 1980s. Third World countries generally believe that enterprises must be tightly controlled. When the home government is dominant in the nexus, state enterprises are discouraged from striking out on their own to expand their market share. Government support for private firms is to add them to the controlled sector. The market economy suffers.

This is an unhealthy view of industrial state enterprise capitalism. It leads to costly, showpiece "cathedrals in the desert" hard to phase down or close because they've become part of the accustomed employment and income base. It is hard to withdraw support to steel mills or auto factories or pharmaceutical plants.

What is most difficult is to turn these controlled sector investments around to make them carry out their commercial activities in line with market requirements—productivity, costs, profitability, and cash flow—in effect, to prune away the nonproductive labor and management structures and commercialize the production system according to the needs of the international market place.

The alternative is to start with and maintain only the loosest controls over state enterprise so that neither government nor enterprise dominates. Then governments intervene in the affairs of firms only at critically important points. For example, they force state- and government-supported firms to combine their commercial interests so the nation-state has one internationally competitive industrial enterprise. France, Canada, The Netherlands, Germany, Norway, Sweden, and now Brazil have adopted this policy. Since the mid-1960s, detailed government intervention has decreased as countries have gained greater confidence that their state enterprises and government-supported firms can help the industrial state prosper.

Nevertheless, this positive attitude depends on success: crude oil, coal, and other resources must flow to the home country. Their flow will be large enough only if the commercial activities of the state enterprise are sufficiently world-wide that they can compete with other multinationals. An increase in total sales to $395 million—large enough to get on the "Fortune 500"—means precious little if the state enterprise is a petroleum firm that must compete with the giants. So a world-wide corporate structure—the state multinational—is the fulcrum for dividing responsibilities within the nexus. With it, this division is relatively easy; without it, this division may even impede the long-term interests of both.

We can already predict that the nexus' power will expand to include manufacturing and agriculture as well as petroleum and minerals. Governments want to regain control over key national resources. They want to have some say in how domestically produced products are sold in multinational situations. We know that new patterns of ownership and new divisions of responsibilities are still to be forthcoming.

The governments of France and Japan loan substantial amounts of debt capital to private firms. When these loans are not repaid, the French translate these into a "blocking minority" equity shareholding, making commercial state enterprises out of once government-supported private firms. The Japanese, who extend a substantially larger proportion of debt capital to their firms, convert the occasional defaults into new loans distributed among those governmental, long-term credit, and *zaibatsu* banks that are bound by fractional ownership, loans, personal loyalties, or long-term buyer-seller relations. This is a different form of state enterprise capitalism, but one that has reaped for Japan strong economic growth at home and virtually unassailable economic power overseas.

We do not know how industrial state enterprise capitalism will accommodate itself to the needs of Third World and socialist countries. Third World countries lack the capability to develop world-scale corporate structures. Their most promising strategy is to purchase controlling stock in private multinationals, thus creating state enterprises in which the government is not the ony shareholder. This form of state enterprise capitalism reveals some of the most instructive issues in the development of the nexus. An outstanding example occurred when Malaysia bought the world's largest tin corporation.

Malaysia's Pernas (or National Concerns, Inc.) is a government-owned financial conglomerate similar to Italy's IRI and Spain's Instituto Nacional de Industria. Between 1974 and 1976, Pernas bought 20 percent of London Tin Corporation on the open market.[6] In 1976, Britain's merchant bank, N. M. Rothschild, worked out a series of complicated takeover maneuvers that the London Stock Exchange's Takeover Panel and the Bank of England approved. Pernas gained control of the Malaysian tin properties of Charter Consolidated Ltd., an associated company of South Africa's Anglo-American Corporation.[7]

These acquisitions, sustained by local attitudes toward industrial statism, reflected a new and impressive adaptation to the goals of state enterprise capitalism. Objections to the outright purchase of stock in the markets of London, Singapore, and Kuala Lumpur came only from the private sector, which realized that foreign governments can use private-sector methods to accomplish public-sector interventionist goals. Private-sector objections to Malaysia's takeover of foreign firms came to a head in late 1976, when Pernas placed three members on Sime Darby's board of directors.[8] It is these takeovers which bring home control over domestic resources, acquire skilled managerial talent, and gain access to overseas market connections. These benefits provide nation-states with a world-scale corporation. Stock purchases are the quickest way for Third World countries, especially the OPEC nations, to invest their capital resources in producing assets well integrated within the international economy.

The number of such acquisitions is still small, because Third World governments still prefer to nationalize industries. But nationalization yields relatively poor results. The confiscations that set up Mexico's Pemex, Chile's Codelco Corporación Nacional del Cobre de Chile, National Copper Corporation of Chile, Argentina's YPF, Zambia's Zimco, Zambia Industrial and Mining Corporation, and Zaire's Gecamines La Generale des Carrieres et des Mines du Zaïre, The General Mining Co. of Zaïre as well as OPEC monopolies failed to improve nation-states' economic power so long as private multinationals controlled the financial, marketing, and management systems. Unless Third World countries and their single-supplier monopolies can gain access to these other systems too, even the most friendly nationalizations will be exercises in futility.

The purchase of common stock should prevent Third World governments from making three big mistakes: (1) extending their countries' limited managerial expertise beyond local capabilities; (2) assuming that today's technologies will be welcome in tomorrow's markets; and (3) above all, dedicating their time to the defense of yesterday's conflicts.

Third World governments purchase stock simply to insure the proper investment of limited new capital. But the prior questions involved are not as simple as they sound: "Which firms are sound investments? Which need to be under local government control? For which do we have the resources to be banker, owner, and manager?"

As we've seen, Britain and Italy didn't think carefully enough about their answers. Sloppy thinking forces governments to invest in "the commanding heights of the economy" rather than to mobilize their resources for investments more appropriate to their cadre of state enterprise managers.

It is pointless to wonder how many Third World governments will buy controlling stock in privately-owned multinationals. Remember instead that home governments wholly own over two-thirds of the fifty-nine state multinational enterprises. This pattern could lead to host governments refusing to let foreign state enterprises invest in their countries unless the local subsidiary has mixed ownership—private and state, foreign and domestic—open to complete integration within domestic industry as managerial expertise grows locally. This would guarantee local control without losing foreign managerial experience and technology.

First, though, we must understand how these partnerships are put together. Particularly, we must clarify the role that state enterprises play in the nexus—how the notion of commercial autonomy works.

Who Handles Business

Commercial autonomy allows the state enterprise to compete with privately-owned firms—to offer customers preferred production and marketing systems, to eliminate obsolete goods and services, and to raise capital without government guarantees. Autonomy is vital for state multinationals, whose big foreign direct investments must show high yields in profits, invested capital, market share, and other commercial objectives. Those from developed countries negotiate state-to-state barter deals for crude oil deliveries. They arrange joint-venture participations at home and abroad as well as the debundling of capital, technology, and marketing services. These debundling contracts permit countries to purchase patent rights to innovations without being forced, as American multinationals often did, to buy management and marketing services too. They set up trading companies with the socialist state enterprises and establish wholly-owned manufacturing subsidiaries in the United States. The state multinationals are practically free to conduct foreign trade and direct investment however they wish, as long as their initiatives strengthen the domestic and foreign economic policies of their home governments.

Since most people associate commercial autonomy with private firms, the organizational structure, business strategy, and work assignments of state enterprises resemble those of private firms. One petroleum state multinational, BP, is a member of the "Seven Sisters"; the others, CFP, Elf-Aquitaine, and ENI, meet all the requirements for joining this Anglo-American club. DSM, VW, and Renault are organized and act like private firms.

These state enterprises are independent for three reasons: (1) state enterprises cannot succeed in a market economy without commercial autonomy; (2) autonomy keeps home governments from diverting the enterprise from its business purpose; and, (3) unless state enterprises have a free hand to deal with microeconomic business activities, governments cannot achieve their foreign economic goals. Sales and profit growth lead to more jobs, higher incomes, increased taxes, and greater economic development.

The state enterprise must be free to make commercial decisions based upon anticipated cost and revenue streams. It must be able to contract for its capital, materials, and supplies and to promise timely delivery of its goods with minimal regard for its sister state enterprises, government-supported firms, and home governments.

Naturally, home governments and their enterprises developed quid pro quo understandings. BP can pour billions of dollars into an American investment knowing that the earnings from its Alaskan oil venture with Sohio will flow into further North Sea exploration. CFP and Elf-Aquitaine spend millions to explore for oil in North America, the Middle East, and Africa, but they know that France has first claim on the crude. VW exports its production and marketing system base to Brazil and South Africa on its own volition but waits until all German government and semiofficial bodies approve its decision to invest in the United States. Commercial autonomy does double duty: it serves both the firm's business policies and the government's foreign economic policies.

There is no precisely-written covenant defining when a home government should intervene, how it should intervene, and who will bear the costs. Instead, the nexus sets up orderly marketing agreements. This strategy lets governments loosen formal controls, assured that enterprises will conform to the national economic plan.

Some state enterprises, particularly the potential multinationals, do carry out specific micro business activities more or less on orders issued by their home governments. For example, Norsk Hydro abandoned its Colorado exploration project because Norway wants it to concentrate its new petroleum investment in the North Sea.[9] Veba took over Gelsenberg on the explicit orders of its government to create a German petroleum state enterprise.[10] And Statsföretag will invest anywhere in Sweden so long as its government lives up to their agreement to subsidize all noncommercial investments in depressed regions of the country.[11] If not limited in their scope, these assignments could hinder these state enterprises from becoming truly multinational firms.

One source of the problem is government expectation about its state enterprises. Brazil recently changed policy, assigning state enterprises new responsibilities: Petrobrás must explore for oil overseas, lift it for use in Brazil, and engage in joint-venture explorations at home. Vale do Rio Doce must adapt its operations similarly. This government spurring for more international trading and investment opportunities is defended as a sacred right. The prerogatives of government, both in law and custom, are great.

The danger is that Third World state enterprises will get their wish—to be exempt from the United Nations Code of Conduct for Transnational Corporations. This would give them a preferred status in foreign markets. This potential benefit does not assure them continued success; similar favors to single-supplier monopolies actually weakened them. The potential multinationals, such as Brazil's two state enterprises, should resist government pressure to seek special favors to subsidize overseas trade and investment. They should not come under the United Nations Code.

How to Maintain Autonomy

The state enterprise also needs to be able to obtain new capital without having to surrender any of its hard-won independence. No government treasury can bargain for control if management uses retained earnings to bargain with private multinational bankers instead. State enterprise profits have made private bankers willing to invest American and Euro-dollars in the rubber underlay and caprolactam technologies of Polysar and DSM, in the marketability of BP's Alaskan crude, and in the exportability of Vale do Rio Doce's iron ore and bauxite. These developments have fundamentally changed the relationship of government to state enterprise.

The state enterprise also needs a stream of innovations which it can offer as competitive alternatives to existing world-scale technology. Not even the most self-confident government minister would substitute judgment on new product development, market positioning, and joint-venture options for that of state enterprise management. In fact, state multinationals—particularly those with investments in the United States—have become skillful in commercializing products from their research and development laboratories.

The remaining danger to state enterprise independence is government threat to rationalize, reorganize or consolidate industrial activities when it decides that domestic firms are not large enough to compete effectively with foreign firms. If government can make a firm multinational by shifting subsidiaries, then it feels little compulsion to maintain existing organizational structures and to speculate upon the future success of current business strategies. State enterprise managers are reluctant to resist, for their work continues whether they are employed as retail gasoline marketers by Norsk Hydro or as chemical salesmen by EMC.

Government intervenes in the affairs of a state enterprise when issues of national economic policy must be decided. A failure of state enterprise management to develop world-scale technology promptly stimulates government to intervene. Such failures force state enterprise managers to jockey for position rather than take care of business. For instance, after Italy dismantled EGAM, Ente Autonomo di Gestione per le Aziende Mineraire Metallurgiche, Autonomous Fiscal Administration for the Mineral-Metallurgical Firm, and assigned its textile and minerals division to ENI, battles over the spoils lasted for years.[12] The British government's attempts to include BNOC in North Sea oil operations has similarly distracted BP from its tasks.

No state enterprise is immune from its home government's will. An enterprise is only as autonomous as it is strong. Before the 1973 OPEC oil crisis, the French petroleum multinationals were more independent than they are now. The French government exercises its influence on the boards of directors through selection of management and through discussions over foreign investments, export of new technologies, and state-to-state deals. Few of the eight state multinationals are as independent as the Swiss and American multinationals, yet their governments nevertheless retain final control over their direction.

Autonomous commercial state enterprises are simply critical to the success of the industrial state because they are inextricably associated with the market economy. In all notable respects the state multinationals are arms of the international economy. This contradicts the accepted doctrine that state enterprises depend upon home governments. Commercial autonomy confirms the nexus' capacity to compete in the world economy.

State enterprise success in gaining commercial autonomy has weakened the will of private firms. It has become easier for them to borrow two-thirds or more of their debt capital from government banks, to accept special grants to hire and retrain the unemployed, to rent low-cost plant and equipment in depressed regions, to give government a "blocking minority" equity interest, and to rationalize their interests with their domestic competitors. Such individual government interventions lead to formal orderly marketing agreements for the industry and to the transformation of private firms to government-supported firms and—once having taken the initial step—to state enterprises.

The threads may now be drawn together. The state enterprise has won a favorable accommodation with government for its commercial needs at the expense of privately-owned business firms. Now state enterprises throughout the world are making private firms an offer they cannot refuse: to work with them in joint business initiatives or face exclusion from markets. And private firms are giving in.

Co-opting Private Firms

State enterprises co-opt private firms mainly in three-party joint ventures among foreign private multinationals, domestic state enterprises, and foreign state multinationals. With the billions Vale do Rio Doce is spending to build Brazilian steel and aluminum industries, this state enterprise has the full support of many Brazilian, American, Canadian, and Japanese private firms as well as that of the Norwegian and Spanish state enterprises. Its array of enticing joint-venture contracts call for each contributor to offer what it can toward the common end of building two strong extractive industries in Brazil. There are good opportunities for continuous supply of iron and bauxite. There are no other ways to gain access to these ores except by providing Vale do Rio Doce with technology, capital, or marketing connections. Given the inevitability of it all, the proper strategy for all foreign firms, private and state, is to find ways to sell their technology, capital, and marketing connections separately and profitably—to serve their own interests as well as those of the local nexus. Since private firms come to identify closely with the specific goals of the Brazilian nexus, they sense the same urgency to bring Third World supply sources into world-scale production.

Private firms that want to open up new markets will search for a state enterprise partner that can guarantee them problem-free acress. This done, the private firms can have something to say about their share of the domestic market, labor costs, taxes, and foreign markets. These will reflect the state enterprise's—and by extension the home government's—goals.

No sharp line separates private firms which support state enterprises and state enterprises themselves. Each commercial organization is important to the other. Their executives migrate between them. Each organization accepts their similar goals. Because of these links, increasingly in the future the state enterprise will be active in international business and will identify with Third World aspirations for power, position, and influence in the world economy. It will enter into joint-venture agreements with other state enterprises, agencies, and government-owned banks as well as with private firms. The state multinational will continue to assume the commercial attributes of its private competitors so that it can compete most effectively in all markets of the world where the nexus wishes to do business.

The state multinationals vitally influence Western market economies. They can participate in the licensing, turnkey services, and equity contracts that count. They can help shape the choice of world-scale technology which, in turn, governs the terms of trade available to Third World countries—e.g., the introduction of DSM's caprolactam process for making nylon in Brazil and the export of the HYL direct reduction process for making sponge steel by Altos Hornos of Mexico to Latin American and Asian countries.[13] State multinationals can have control over alienation of the world's petroleum and mineral resources and shape the supply conditions for their use in the developed world. Finally, they can help bring socialist state enterprises into closer working relationships with the market-sector state enterprises, thereby reshaping beliefs and assumptions about the international economic order for years to come.

Co-opting Socialist State Enterprises

Market-sector state enterprises render services on the international front in vast and increasing volume. Recently they have forged ties with the socialist countries of Eastern Europe. By any applicable test, their socialist enterprises are outside the market economy when they do business at home, but they enter into tangential market relationships with other countries. For instance, Yugoslavia agreed to let Renault build assembly facilities, set up switch houses to sell their automobile parts in Third World countries, and buy their engines to install in French-made Renaults.

Not only has state enterprise capitalism accepted socialist exports to the West, but it has also permitted socialist enterprises to be established in all western nations, including the United States itself.

For example, DAL, a $300 million Polish foreign trade firm, owns twenty-eight subsidiaries in fifteen Western countries; Hungarotex, a $500 million Hungarian textile export-import firm, has joint venture subsidiaries in France, Germany, Italy, and The Netherlands; and Avtoexport, a $1.3 billion Russian auto exporter, finances, owns, and manages commercial enterprises in the West. In 1976, the Russian maritime-shipping ministry, Sovinflot, established Morflot American Shipping Inc. (Moram), headed by an American executive, to seek out American customers for the Russian maritime fleet. Its annual business volume is already $70 million.[14]

Socialist firms are growing and maturing in the world economy. For instance, Dal acquired a $20 million loan from the First National Bank of Chicago without a government guarantee.[15] As their commercial activities become vital to certain industrial states, the market-sector state enterprises seek them out to confirm their own importance to their home governments.

The commercial influence of state enterprises, market or socialist, extends to shaping the legal rules under which they can do business in Western nations. Except in England, state enterprises are no longer granted sovereign immunity protection in courts of the developed countries.[16] Even as branches of the national government from which they spring, these state enterprises can be sued in American courts for their commercial acts.[17]

The shift in commercial power has been profound. The private multinational is feared for its past conquests and honored for its current market prowess, but its economic influence has dwindled. The state enterprise, as the commercial agent of a more powerful political nexus, has gained ground in a climate of belief that it can do economic justice to countries long victimized in the international economy. Rising Third World socialist influence will nurture new distributions of power, new divisions of responsibilities, and new views of commercial autonomy.

10

Foreign Economic Relations

IN THE 1950s, managers of industrial state enterprises found their hands tied. Their firms were small-scale, wasteful monopolies used as investment vehicles to solve long-standing, intractable economic problems.

When America accelerated its foreign direct investment during the 1960s, Western European and some Third World countries cut some strings and forced their state enterprises to become commercial state enterprises—to compete. Industrial state enterprise capitalism generated sharply rising world sales. Government-owned and -supported commercial corporations grew like Topsy, diversifying and multiplying joint ventures and direct investments overseas.

Management policy focused on strategic corporate planning. It guided the pace and direction of corporate growth from domestic state enterprise to important international firm to potential multinational and finally to state multi-national enterprise. Basic international business strategies—exports versus investments, assemblies versus full line production, sales service versus complete marketing-mix support, and debt and equity financing versus switch house arrangements—changed to support foreign economic policies. The fifty-nine state enterprises were ready to compete forcefully in the world economy.

Compared with the performance of the non-American private firms, the achievement of the fifty-nine state enterprises is impressive. From 1971 to 1976, enterprises achieved a 21.0 percent compound annual growth rate for sales compared with 10.1 percent for the private firms (Table A–4 in Appendix). Moreover, petroleum state enterprises and extractive state enterprises grew faster than their equivalent number in the private sector in growth sales and assets (Table A–14 in Appendix).

Even more striking is the pattern of emerging dominance of state enterprises over non-American private firms. From column 1 of Table A–6 in the Appendix we see the obvious shift to state enterprise dominance in the petroleum industry from 1971 to 1976. Equally obvious, state enterprises in the extractive industries (column 2) have compound annual growth rates from 29 to 66 percent greater than the growth rates of the private firm group. This pattern is repeated to a lesser degree in the automobile industry.

Column 5 suggests that the growth of the average state enterprise is a larger multiple of the growth of the average private firm. Sales of the average state enterprise grew at 2.08 times the compound annual growth rate of sales of the average non-American private firm, and assets and net income growth rates had equally large multiples of the private firm rates.

134

The recent economic achievement of commercial state enterprises follows largely from national policies that have enhanced sales and asset growth. The nexus of the 1970s has begun to benefit from the income potential of these enterprises. It may be a pivotal event for capitalism. At least, it signals a major change of the world's political economy into a pluralistic business community in which the state enterprise is another effective international firm.

National and corporate plans are the link to social and commercial objectives. By forecasting costs, revenues, and impact upon local industry and incomes, the nexus allocates sectors of the economy for domestic state enterprise control, for joint government-owned and government-supported enterprise commercialization, or for domestic and foreign enterprise participation. North American, European, African, Asian, and Latin American countries refuse to let foreign private and state enterprises decide these matters.

Americans don't really believe such organized use of the nexus exists. They kid themselves in believing that market-sector state enterprises are just like private firms and will stand or fall on their market performance. When someone points out how the federal government bails out large-scale operations like Lockheed and set up transportation state enterprises—Conrail and Amtrak—hardly anyone listens. Those examples are seen as temporary aberrations, nothing like the industrial state enterprises set up by foreign governments or their manufacturing subsidiaries in the United States.

It all seems implausible and therefore we don't demand reciprocity. And we forget the nexus is a competing political force in the world economy.

For a variety of reasons, some grounded in myth, others

in suspicion of foreign ideologies, America refuses to consider linking government and business in order to compete against this new socioeconomic organization. After all, we claim, free enterprise is the best possible way to organize the economy, therefore a race between private and government-owned firms is no contest.

When local private firms falter, American businessmen blame "too much government intervention." Note the germ of truth within the misunderstanding. It is foreign government intervention—from equity ownership to debt capital support for domestic market control and overseas market penetration—that pushes American firms to the wall. But American government intervention on behalf of American firms could be beneficial. These businessmen forget that there are goods, some of them very capital-intensive, that cannot be produced at all unless government provides the funds, sets up local factories, and creates a marketing system. While recognizing that local private firms can't afford large risks, governments also abhor the thought of surrendering economic sovereignty to foreign firms. So should we. Their solution: the state multinational. If host countries were to recognize that these foreign state investors are a threat— something we haven't done—they wouldn't hesitate to use all the powers of national sovereignty to protect the local economy and its firms.

Germany Counters French Threat

In 1969, Germany recognized the threat of the French nexus by refusing CFP permission to take over Gelsenberg.[1] The prospective merger into a continental corporation would have countered Anglo-American petroleum firms, but French leadership would have put the enterprise outside of Germany's orderly marketing agreements. Germany would merely have substituted French for Anglo-American petroleum hegemony.

When OPEC forced Germany's hand, Veba received a new mission and a new subsidiary. Together Veba and Gelsenberg (a former government-supported private firm) are to negotiate state-to-state barter deals with the Arab states, supply crude oil to Germany, and become petroleum state multinational.[2]

Canadian Nexus at Work

The Canadian nexus has carried out several key policies. First, the federal government set up CDC to counter the American challenge north of the 49th parallel. The Dominion set new federal policy on foreign direct investment and passed federal and provincial laws permitting national and provincial state enterprises which could enter into joint ventures with American petroleum and mineral firms. The CDC itself, its Polysar subsidiary, the Alberta Energy Corporation, and several American firms invested $430 million in the new petrochemical plant in Sarnia, Ontario.[3] This gave Canada a way to supply Polysar's rubber-mixing acquisitions in the United States.

Second, as we've seen, CDC bought Polysar's American subsidiaries to create a way to curtail American market position for rubber-mixing products in Canada. Together with the Texasgulf takeover, this is the Canadian nexus at work.

Third, the Canadian government is buying back all foreign air frame manufacturers in order to create a single Canadian air frame producer capable of competing in world markets.[4]

Fourth, CDC is supposed to create an internationally competitive health care and pharmaceutical industry. Therefore it is buying up Canadian laboratories and making joint-venture investments in Brazil.[5]

Finally, Canada has charged Petro-Canada and CDC-Oil with making Canada's petroleum policy as independent as possible.[6]

OPEC Challengers

OPEC countries recognize that their oil reserves are an important weapon to wrest market power from the "Seven Sisters" and the United States and British governments. Posted price policy and availability of crude are linked to the West's policy toward Israel, the inflationary rise in the price of manufactured goods from the West, and what the West will do to change its trade policies toward Third World countries.

The OPEC monopolies collaborate with their home governments. Petromin of Saudi Arabia, National Iranian Oil, Petroven of Venezuela, Nigerian Oil, and others are joint-venture partners in all energy-related investments in their home countries. They provide capital to such pan-Arab projects as the sugar investments in the Sudan and managerial talent to Ecuador's petroleum state enterprise, Cepe.[7] Petroven (Petróleos Venezolanos, Venezuelan Petroleum Co.) and Petrobrás compete for favors from Colombia's petroleum state enterprise, Ecopetrol (Empresa Colombiana de Petróleos, Colombian Petroleum Co.).[8] Argentina's YPF competes against Venezuela's Petroven to explore in Ecuador and against Petrobrás in Bolivia for lifting agreements.[9]

Third World nexuses are following the lead of developed countries through acquisitions, new investments, and expanded trade. Iran bought Germany's Krupp; Libya bought into Fiat; Kuwait and Dubai bought into Lonhro; Malaysia took over London Tin and Sime Darby. And the National Iranian Oil Company has twice begun negotiations with Ashland Oil and Shell Oil to buy retail marketing capacity in the United States.[10]

No longer are the "Seven Sisters" the only guilty party in forestalling competition in petroleum. Every country organizes its nexus to give its own petroleum state firms preference in its home market and seeks to negotiate collaborative state-to-state barter deals and parallel-purchase agreements to insure access to scarce crude, marketing connections, and managerial talents. Any two nexuses arrange their petroleum affairs to suit their own needs.

Predictions

Viewing the nexus in purely international business terms, we can draw some important conclusions about the future political economy of the world.

1. Direct investments without links to foreign or local state enterprises and government-supported firms will rarely work, for developed and less-developed countries alike oppose foreign takeovers. If state enterprise capitalism does

not play its role, the nexus will not develop and state enterprises will not perform. Capital flow will continue to diminish because perceptions of profit and risk have changed. Agreements about the use of world-scale technology, marketing connections, and managerial talent will stall.

2. As Third World countries increase their collective power, joint ventures will become the norm because the developed countries and their state enterprises also favor them. They involve lower capital exposure and less risk, they will reduce conflicts with host governments, and they provide favors—reduced competition and specialized state financing. Indeed, as important as joint ventures are to the Third World countries, they are perhaps even more important to the developed countries. As overseas investments generate market advantages and tie resources and foreign distribution systems to the parent firm, the nation-state becomes stronger in the world market.

Countries used to assume that foreign direct investments meant that foreign firms would own and control capital, technology, marketing, and executive talent. It was a matter of all or nothing, take-it-or-leave-it. These nation-states remained outside the flows of international commerce, as isolated as the socialist countries of Eastern Europe. The private multinationals dominated the choices: they wanted wholly-owned subsidiaries, they preferred complete control, and they kept their technology and marketing connections secret.

The ethos of international business has changed. Local governments want low-cost or free access to technology. They expect foreign firms to tie them into distant marketing connections. They insist that their state enterprises break down the competitive advantage held by foreign firms. They insist that local people be trained in all aspects of the business. The current ethos is to separately sell all elements of the foreign investment contract so the nexus can buy what it wants and from whom it pleases.

In recent years, suppliers of resources and services from the developed countries have responded to Third World pressures by offering investment packages more suitable to less-developed countries, and suppliers from Third World and socialist countries have been offering their own investment packages. The promising course is that the host country will receive the lowest possible bid. State enterprises promise to build this strategy into a major alternative to traditional international business efforts.

Foreign Investment Guidelines

The purposes of state enterprise capitalism are identical with the domestic policy established by countries to bring in foreign investors under strict guidelines. The foreign firm that wants to continue its full ownership of a local firm must divest portions of its equity over a certain period of time or face loss of that local market altogether. This is the intent of the Andean Pact and the Nigerianization of industry. Third World countries especially cannot ignore flows of capital, technology, and marketing connections between developed and less developed regions. These should be in support of their national economic policies.

Having gained control over foreign investments at home, these governments are ready to compete in foreign markets themselves. This expansion is essential in a world where international business success is the highest forum for commercial admiration.

The impact of the nexus upon the host country should be important to Americans. Some of our citizens already depend economically on state enterprise management's choices on wages and prices. Since state enterprise management goals are not confined to making the highest profits possible, their choices can have large effects. Coal and petroleum may be kept here or sent abroad, earnings may be reinvested here or repatriated, and America may be used as an export base or be closed out of markets.

The important lessons of the 1970s is that governments should develop foreign economic policies which include large responsibilities for state enterprises overseas. When tied carefully to domestic economic policies, these substantially serve the needs of the nation-state. An example that principally affects us is the French and German governments decision to use CDF and Veba as the national firms responsible for finding coal for national industries. Veba spent $24 million to gain control over subsidiary mining interests in West Virginia.[11] The mines never stopped producing coal, but now it is put on unit-trains bound for Norfolk, Virginia and the export shipping lanes to Europe.

The United States never questioned the government-state enterprise linkage in this foreign direct investment, even though coal is a depletable resource that we may need for our own energy needs. Indeed, the majority of state enterprise investments in the United States tend to pursue foreign economic needs at the expense of American interests. The continuing saga of BP's alienation of Alaskan oil opens up many more possibilities. The managements of some forty international state enterprises have numerous lawful and unexploited opportunities to grab stakes in America's petroleum, coal, potash, phosphate, and timber.

Moreover, the managements of some ninety-two international government-supported firms have even more possibilities for taking over American resources and firms. These commercial incentives also serve the needs of the nation-state. An example that affects us is the Japanese government's commitment of $250 million to their electronics firms. Fujitsu and Hitachi, two of Japan's top semiconductor and computer manufacturers, are seeking out the secrets of American high-technology electronics as part of Japan's Very Large Scale Integration Program to gain dominance of the world's computer and electronics markets. Plants (and their talented employees) in the San Francisco Bay area are being taken over as these government-supported firms seek to master the latest technology now understood only by American firms.

The United States never questioned the home government—government-supported firm linkage in this foreign direct investment, even though American technological leadership may disappear. Indeed, government-supported firms' investments in the United States tend to pursue foreign economic needs at the expense of American interests. The alignment of France's Pechiney with Alumax, itself a joint venture of AMAX and Mitsui, suggests that predictions about international business are even coming true in the United States.

In all the arrangements that arouse alarm today, there is none as difficult to accept as the deliberate attempt by a state enterprise to build an American manufacturing base in order to curtail the hard-won position of American firms in the home country of the government-owned firm. With the emergence of five potential state multinationals and their strong commitment to the habits of state enterprise capitalism, the danger increases. For the modern state multinational does indeed have the power to shape the American economy—a power that comes in part from its own success as an international corporation, in part from its close working tie with its home government.

The real purpose of this power is to serve the deeper interests of the society from which these firms spring. These goals are neither widely-known nor understood in the United States.

Government and Enterprise Share
Investment Decisions

Most European governments have preferred foreign direct investments where these will do them the most political good—cementing former colonial ties, making certain key Third World countries favor them with resources, and securing a foothold in the European Common Market. Deciding to invest in the United States directs scarce capital away from markets of greater need to a highly-developed mass-consumption market which can yield a higher return on invested capital. It is a high-risk decision made more so by political instability in countries with the greatest need for capital. It presents political problems for government, leading to change in the home government's view of its state enterprises.

The investment decision is far too important to be made by the state enterprise alone. If the firm is going to compete internationally, this decision must be based on a conscious choice among cost and revenue alternatives rather than on favoritism for former territories, desire for unimpeded access to Arab oil, or on prestige for penetrating markets of neighboring countries.

How the Consensus Works

The investment experiences of CFP and Elf-Aquitaine illustrate this shared power over the direction of foreign direct investment. France considers its two petroleum state multinationals to be independent of government and therefore able to "conduct their own policies;" Algeria ridicules this public statement.[12] In 1975, these two enterprises took opposite positions in dealing with Sonatrach, Algeria's petroleum and natural gas single-supplier monopoly.

CFP, considered more independent of France in its international operations, expanded its oil accord with Sonatrach by agreeing to take 43 percent more crude and drilling many more new wells both in the Sahara and offshore in the Mediterranean.

Elf-Aquitaine refused to renew its agreement with Sonatrach. Elf cited that the required research and development conditions are tantamount to raising the price for Algerian crude above its posted price.

One state enterprise had not been successful in altering its dependence on North African crude, while the other had substituted Gabonese and Iraqi oil for the oil from Algeria. Through Elf, the French government told Algeria that when other sources become available France will shift its purchases elsewhere, unless price and other terms are reasonable, regardless of sentimental ties with former colonies. Elf achieved this success only when it had considered where it should make its foreign direct investments and stopped depending fully upon oil from one source, the Algerian Sahara.

Traditionally, both Elf and CFP had defined their foreign direct investments in terms of France's past. This proved to be unsatisfactory when Algeria increased royalty payments, raised its own share of profits, required production-sharing agreements, and nationalized oil. Realizing that they must diversify their sources of oil, both state enterprises joined in the search for North Sea oil (in both the Norwegian and British sectors), for crude from Alberta, and for oil and gas from the Louisiana Gulf Coast.[13] This meant switching from the France-Algerian connection to the France-North Atlantic connection. In the Gaullist past, this would never have been considered. In the present, it is an appropriate strategy to give France added oil security.

The French petroleum industry also realizes it must sell its oil products in new markets rather than expecting the French government to raise domestic gasoline prices high enough to cover the new posted prices and higher costs of transportation and refining. These firms are building up production and marketing systems in Great Britain, where they bought British and American domestic systems, and in Canada and the United States, where they gained a foothold with takeovers and new investments.[14] Today, both French state multinationals manage fully-integrated North American petroleum businesses. Their American subsidiaries report to management located in Alberta. The difference between a headquarters in Calgary and one in Houston amounts to very little, for ultimate power lies in Paris, where government interacts with business to sustain France.

Both the French government and the two state enterprises realized early that different responses to the same foreign situation are quite appropriate if government and enterprises are to achieve their most sought-after goal— guaranteeing France's access to the lowest-cost fuel possible. From the start, the French state firms have analyzed their options, calculated their cost and revenue streams, and chosen new markets with care.

One of the great strengths of state enterprise over private enterprise is now apparent. Although government and the corporation may have different concepts of what is needed and what should be done, they can work out a compromise which is at least mutually satisfying—and over the long run, much more than that.

PART FOUR

Nexus Strategies

11

Investments in the United States

AMERICAN ADVOCATES of a "live and let live" policy believe that the American manufacturing subsidiaries of foreign state enterprises can be absorbed into the economy of the United States without seriously impairing our free enterprise business management system. They are wrong: state enterprise capitalism is not easy to absorb. It is a sea change—a fundamental change in the character of the international economy and those national economies which encounter its orderly marketing agreements.

The commercial autonomy granted to many state enterprises, particularly to the eight state multinationals and the five potential multinationals, has yielded substantial economic benefits. In 1976, the combined sales of commercial state enterprises were $185 billion; combined assets totaled $176 billion. As Table A–7 (in Appendix) shows, "state enterprises have come to dominate the top 100 even more than they dominate the 500. . . . A comparison of average enterprise growth rates . . . suggests that it is this 'edging out' (of non-American private firms in the top 100) . . . which explains the increasing dominance of state enterprises in the top 100."[1]

"Should we invest in the United States?"

Each state enterprise must face this decision. From it flow managerial actions about organizational structure, business strategies, and executive assignments. The manager must weigh the costs and benefits of investments here against those in Germany, Canada, Australia, and South Africa. He must convert his firm's technologies and marketing connections into commercial ventures acceptable to both Third World and socialist countries. Finally, he must think through how to make decisions today that will permit the firm to outperform competitors in years to come.

Why Invest in America?

In order to increase the profitability of their American operations, the state multinationals combine resources, capital, and managerial talent into competitive market strategies. Their prospects for success improve as they convince Americans to buy Total gasoline, DSM caprolactam, Polysar latex, and VW Rabbits.

The more state enterprises adopt multinational organizational structures, the more likely they are to invest in the United States. Unified corporate strategies allow them to transfer information across national boundaries and open our market. Their top managements focus on integrating American subsidiaries into world-wide corporate plans—to contribute to the performance of their European and Canadian parent enterprises.

Foreign direct investment adds a significant new dimension, adding resources available to feed established production and marketing systems and generating innovations to be parlayed as products for world markets. At the same time, the world firm increasingly depends upon success in the American market. Preferring to buy well-established production and marketing systems rather than set them up from scratch, state enterprises have shown they are no different from privately-owned multinationals in their preferred route for making a direct investment in the United States.

The information state enterprise managers are receiving is simply that American business is for sale. They should be hearing instead that we'd prefer they set up a new manufacturing facility. After all, American customers are constantly defining new market opportunities. By the time an established firm's problems are worked out and it is integrated into the world-wide enterprise, it may be too late to take advantage of these new markets. Unless a state firm is ready beforehand with a market base to distribute its exports, a production base to produce its new technologies, and an organizational system to manage its American subsidiaries, no quick purchase of a domestic firm will make an American investment profitable. We should encourage foreign managers to consider a range of options from purchasing existing factories to establishing new "grass-roots" plants so that they can maximize returns on investments.

In some cases—particularly when the investment is in

153

energy, minerals or other natural resources—we should encourage joint ventures as Canada does. For example, Spain's
Instituto Nacional de Industria manages mining exploration
and development for its partner, Société Quebeçoise d'Exploration, in St. Foy, Quebec.[2] Finland's Enso Gutzeit and
Kymi Kymmene (a government-supported private firm)
provide timber to a sawmill in British Columbia which is
jointly owned with Weldwood of Canada, a subsidiary of
Champion Paper, which will manage and market the lumber
products.[3]

In making the shift from partner to manager, a state
enterprise must have enough control over a firm so that the
chief executive officer of a small domestic firm becomes the
viceroy of a foreign government-owned firm in the United
States. The foreign investor which looks for the right American firm to buy into first takes a controlling position in it
and then, by providing clear guidelines about what it expects
from its managers, it can make the American subsidiary
profitable.

One example is the petroleum subsidiary built in Michigan, Illinois, and Wisconsin by CFP around its purchase
of Leonard Refineries of Alma, Michigan. In 1966, CFP
paid $6.8 million for a one-third share of Leonard.[4] Leonard's
president, Reid Brazell, favored the transaction and continued as chief executive officer. The foreign parent watched
Leonard's net income drop by 44 percent in the next two
years. In 1970, it paid an additional $12.6 million for the
remaining shares of Leonard,[5] replaced Reid Brazell with two
new managers,[6] and integrated all of its North American
operations by changing all Leonard stations in Michigan
and Illinois and all Martin stations in Wisconsin to Total
stations, the world brand name of CFP.

Acquisitions Promote State
Enterprise Capitalism

Exactly why are investments in the United States so attractive?

The record provides a clue. While it is necessary to make foreign direct investments here in order to become truly multinational, state enterprises have the additional special goal of benefiting the industrial statism of individual countries. Four diverse reasons for state enterprises to use America to strengthen state capitalism illustrate this complex phenomenon.

The first reason is to have a secure source of raw materials. We have no record of nationalization, expropriation, or takeovers. We do not impede a foreign firm's right to mine ore or to sell or export it to whomever it pleases. But three European state enterprises—Veba, CDF, and BP—are using their control over our minerals to improve their world position.

We should not take this lightly. If we don't develop a policy toward these investments, our relative abundance in resources will become geared to European and Japanese industrial needs. When the need for their use at home arises, as it will before the turn of the century, we will be unable to restrict exports of coal without major diplomatic disputes. Especially coal—good coking coal, easily mined coal, coal for making electrical power, and coal to last from 100 to 20 years when oil and gas have long run out.

In 1974, CDF and two French government-supported private firms (Usinor and Schneider) paid Belco Petroleum

$36 million for 80 percent of Hawley Coal Mining Corporation, giving the French control over six West Virginia coal mines and others in Kentucky.[7] The relative change in American and French economic power, with its uncertain definitions and its shifting boundaries, creates an opportunity for CDF to raise its level of coal imports from the United States substantially beyond its current figure of 2.8 million tons annually.[8] We can expect CDF to secure most of France's needed 17 percent increase in coal for the next decade from American mines.[9]

Germany, Italy, and Britain see these French investments in America as a multinational challenge, possibly crucial to the whole international economic structure for competition over "the world product." France threatens to hinder their access to American resources, even to become independent of Western Europe. Since this is, above all, a test of the international effectiveness of French state capitalism, the others follow France to America.

The Hugo Stinnes subsidiary of Veba, in a joint venture with Ruhrkohle, paid $24 million for the Appalachian Resources Company—coal mines producing 900,000 tons annually in Kentucky and West Virginia.[10] Appalachian Resources' estimated reserves of between 77 and 120 million tons ensure West Germany's future supply of metallurgical coal.

BP entered the American coal industry by acquiring Sohio's Old Ben Coal Company, whose mines at West Frankfurt, Illinois, and Oakland, Indiana, produce 7 million tons annually.[11] Elf-Aquitaine became the owner of anthracite and bituminous coal mines in Pennsylvania when it took over Westrans Industries.[12] These state multinationals are diversifying away from complete dependence on oil by buying American mines and leasing federal and privately-owned lands to explore for other ores.

The habit of letting foreign government-subsidized enterprises take control over American mines has become very commonplace and we do not give it second thought. However, in addition to the 1920 policy of reciprocity, we have a 1948 attorney general's ruling that Britain is no longer reciprocal with respect to coal. This ruling, prepared when Britain set up the National Coal Board, did not envision a huge petroleum state enterprise becoming a coal investor as well. Yet we must watch out, or this kind of diversification will be considered irrelevant to the policy of reciprocity. Petroleum state enterprises cannot profit forever from lifting and marketing petroleum. Like privately-owned firms, they are seeking new agreements to insure their own international corporate survival and to assure a steady supply of resources to their home countries.

The second reason for investing in the United States is that state enterprises have valuable resources to sell to American consumers. Their executives believe that these products are unique and that a strong market can be established in the United States.

For DSM this new product is caprolactam. This technological innovation allows the raw material for nylon to be produced without infringing on Du Pont's patents. Since nylon markets had already been developed, DSM could undersell Du Pont by producing cheaper raw material, and its process would become the world's standard, or at least the standard in Third World countries, which want lower-cost technologies from the developed countries. As we shall see, the managers of DSM used all the sophisticated business strategies at their command to develop markets for caprolactam both in the developed and Third World countries.

The same is true for government-supported, privately-owned firms. For France's Pechiney Ugine Kuhlman this new product is a primary reduction process for aluminum. This technological innovation uses 20 percent less power than standard American reduction technology. Since power costs loom large in the total costs of aluminum, Pechiney and its partners (AMAX and Mitsui) can undersell Alcoa, Reynolds, and other large primary producers. Managers of Pechiney have parlayed their energy-saving discovery into operating companies around the world, making the parent firm a prime contender to oust privately-owned multinationals from capitalizing on new aluminum demand in the Third World.

A third reason for investing in the United States is to have enough resources to supply the new market position. For example, CFP has lacked adequate supplies of American crude. Without important new finds at the wells it was drilling in the United States, it would be unable to provide crude for its refinery, terminals, and gas stations. This led it to pay $36.4 million for a major drilling operator, the Hanover Petroleum Corporation.[13] Elf-Aquitaine is also moving aggressively to buy out crude suppliers, such as Pruett & Hughes, Westrans, and Coastal States Gas Corporation to supply its American and Canadian distribution system.[14]

The fourth reason for investing in the United States is to oust American industries from market dominance. The nexus' government wants to end American multinational control over its home market. We spoke earlier about how Polysar's rubber-tubing investment, if successful, would reduce our firms' access to Canadian markets. And we noted how Japanese semiconductor and computer firms are waging a relentless battle in California to acquire resources so they will wrest dominance away from America. Both government-owned and government-supported firms are out to replace us in the most important markets of the world.

The Results

These four reasons for investments in the United States have proved valid. To build their competitive strength, state enterprises must attract large amounts of capital to finance the sale of their products through marketing connections they alone will use.

American bankers lent BP $1.7 billion to put the Sohio marketing system at the service of Alaskan oil and transform a regional jobber into a fully-integrated petroleum corporation.[15] This is a marketing management innovation of immense proportions, far outweighing anything any other foreign state enterprise has done in America. So far the BP-Sohio team has marketed itself well in the private capital markets of the United States.

Besides private placement, a state enterprise can sell shares in its American subsidiary at a public offering. The stock of CFP's Canadian subsidiary was already traded on the AMEX, Toronto, and Montreal exchanges before it bought Leonard Refineries. In 1973, when an additional $15 million was needed to finance further acquisitions, exploration, and development, the Canadian subsidiary made a public offering of 3.5 million shares and sold it down to the "tag ends."[16]

The management of capital supply is important to the

petroleum and minerals state enterprises because they are highly capital-intensive firms. Setting objectives for financing the sale and distribution of their products is crucial to international economic success. Yet no international banker will provide funds unless these state firms have a well-conceived plan to make something of their investments in the United States.

The Canadian government set up the CDC with an initial capitalization of $250 million. No additional funds were promised. Unless the enterprise made money on its initial supply of capital, no private banker would take its notes. It had to invest in Canadian businesses that provided it with a yield equal to or higher than alternative uses. For the top management team of CDC, the condition which makes this state enterprise different from all other federal and provincial crown corporations is that the firm has to earn its way by marketing its worth as a capital user. Their enterprise will not remain outside the crown corporation framework unless profits remain high enough to obtain additional injections of capital.

Within eighteen months of acquiring control over Texasgulf, CDC transferred its Texasgulf shares to a new Dutch subsidiary, CDC Nederlands BV.[17] The United States tax treaty with Holland permits Dutch companies which own 25 percent or more of an American firm to withhold five percent on dividends paid rather than the usual 15 percent. There is no withholding under the Canadian-Dutch tax treaty. Thus CDC increased its net income from Texasgulf by 11.8 percent from $9.5 million to $10.6 million in 1975. This is a perfect flow-through, a brilliant financial maneuver among a web of tax treaties.

This tax dodge will promote more foreign investment by

CDC and its American subsidiaries. Polysar will be a prime beneficiary, raising its $30 million investment to new highs. CDC will also take over more American firms in Canada; CDC Oil & Gas Ltd. will benefit as it adds other petroleum firms to its Tenneco properties in Alberta.[18] Finally, CDC may use the maneuver to invest outside North America. The pharmaceuticals-health care complex that CDC is trying to assemble in Canada through the purchase of Omnimedic and Connaught Medical Research Laboratories and in Third World countries through joint ventures with Denmark's Dumex in Brazil could mean increased competition for American firms that sell health-care products to state enterprise distributors in Italy, Brazil, and elsewhere.[19]

In a relatively short time, CDC is sloughing off its unilateral commitment to the Canadian market. It plans to use the tax-free resources it generates from its Texasgulf investment to build a Canadian presence in the major growth markets of the world and to do this at the expense of entrenched American firms.

The most important time to ask seriously "Should we invest in the United States?" is when the domestic state enterprise is successful at home. Understanding this has been the great strength of the state multinationals, not only in their investments here but in their direct investments elsewhere. Success at home makes the commercial behavior of domestic state enterprises obsolete. It forces these firms to look abroad, to see the future as multinationals.

The quest to be multinational is equally important as a reason for foreign investment. Montedison, the state multinational with the least commitment to overseas markets, has decided to change its international image. Over the last few years, it bought Novamont, a polypropylene plant in

West Virginia, and Swedcast, an acrylic sheet plant in Kentucky; it built the CNA nitrate plant in The Netherlands; it went into joint ventures in Belgium, England, and Spain; and it licensed its technology and helped build twenty-two plants in Eastern Europe and the Third World.[20] The potential multinationals are following the same pattern. Such investment requires manufacturing and marketing options in all the developed countries and in many Third World countries as well. The government-supported private firms (such as France's Saint-Gobain-Pont-à-Mousson, Germany's Fried. Krupp, and Japan's Mitsubishi) are using government loans and guarantees to make the same multinational commitment to the American market. What starts out as a new product from the home market becomes a whole family of new products for many different markets.

For example, DSM—once a coal company—has penetrated European and world markets by developing caprolactam, lysene for cattle feed, and other new technologies. By the early 1960s, it branched out to the United States, first producing fertilizer, then caprolactam. The firm's decision to invest in America instead of in The Netherlands countered the prevailing European fear of the American market. Today DSM has subsidiaries and affiliates in all major world markets and licenses its technology where it cannot own subsidiaries. By the mid-1970s it became more certain that state enterprises need the American market to smooth out their business-cycle problems. These multinational dynamics are at work for many other state enterprises investing in the United States, Canada, and the rest of the developed world.

BP was already multinational before buying Sohio. It needed a domestic distribution system to market Alaskan oil. Given the continuation of high OPEC prices, it expects its American petroleum business to cover costs of getting oil out of Alaska. It also expects Sohio to provide a stream of revenues for the British government to use for North Sea drilling. BP's investment is in fact a search for raw materials, a drive for market position, a device for profit, and a means of becoming more multinational.

Foreign direct investment by state and government-supported enterprises is a complex phenomenon. As we have seen, some of the pressures that bring about this investment are clear-cut; others are not. Some, such as the search for raw materials, are induced by foreign governments' fear of a reduced share of the division of "the world product." In some cases, the driving force behind the foreign investment is the state enterprise itself, seeking to keep up with its business competitors by building market position and integrating backwards towards suppliers. The combination of government desire for economic power with enterprise need for market position makes their foreign direct investments an immense and difficult problem for America.

12

Organizing the Production System

STATE ENTERPRISE MANAGERS are responsible for investing in promising markets or divesting from unpromising markets. They must link parent and subsidiary enterprises in strategies to promote exports, foreign direct investments, joint mineral sourcing agreements, coproduction deals, and other international commercial arrangements. They must also make key decisions such as: (1) the selection of local executives; (2) the choice of products to sell in new markets; (3) the size of the production and marketing system to be put in place; (4) the competition of subsidiaries for expansion rights in Third World countries; (5) the allocation of assignments between executives of the parent and subsidiary enterprises; (6) the choice of business strategies for penetrating markets not now served by the multinational corporation.

Organizing the Production System

One reason that Americans have not fully grasped the gathering strength of state enterprise capitalism is that until now, hardly anyone has appreciated what state enterprise managers have accomplished in the United States and elsewhere. We can, though, now chart both the substantial accomplishments and how they were achieved.

Organizing Leadership

State enterprises are beginning to succeed in hiring good managers because they now demand entrepreneurial skills and offer an opportunity for a manager to operate a well-functioning production and marketing system which yields a high return on capital for the parent firm.

VW sought someone to run a fully-integrated manufacturing operation, and most importantly, someone who had start-up experience in building a new automobile factory in the United States. To get this man—James W. McLernon, a former GM executive—VW top management had to convince him that he would be building a new auto empire which eventually would have plants throughout the United States and Canada and would be manufacturing and selling 500,000 cars annually.

All McLernon had to begin with was the tattered sales and distribution system built by Stuart Perkins, an Englishman, to service 500,000 imports. When McLernon arrived, this marketing organization was servicing half that amount, and its dealers were selling other imported models as well, something VW had avoided until then.[1] This system is now being merged with the top, middle, and lower line manage-

165

ment, planning staff, and production-line personnel that McLernon brought in from other American auto firms.

In contrast, BP left the production and marketing system of Sohio in place. From the beginning, Sohio's chairman, Charles Spahr, and his top management team have been the best set of American executives BP could find for its new subsidiary. The team's private placement of $1.2 billion for Sohio and another $500 million for BP—itself a part of the $5 billion debt and equity addition to Sohio's capital structure—has been outstanding.[2] The team's ability to fend off new Congressional controls and shunt aside local politics in Alaska has shown its worth.

The team is concerned with pipeline policy both in Alaska and from the West Coast to the Midwest, and with turning its oil into profitable downstream businesses. It is trying to get the dividends from Alaskan oil to flow to BP, knowing full well that these profits will not be plowed back into Sohio's American petroleum and coal businesses. In the end, Charles Spahr and his team may be seen as the villains. They let a substantial part of the only major source of new American crude fall into the hands of a foreign multinational nexus to use in building production capacity in the North Sea.

The cry for a change in management is more common, as in the French handling of all their investments here. Their firms are no more immune than others from the failure of foreigners who are trained to accept government tutelage and who can't understand that the American government simply regulates business but rarely enters into partnership with it. It is absurd to expect that only Frenchmen can manage American subsidiaries. If these firms follow the worst examples of American firms overseas, their state enterprises will likely fail in the battle for market position in the United States and Canada.

The most sophisticated organizational arrangement is to combine the two propositions: create an entity with ties to both the Old and New Worlds. To say, as DSM does in its advertising, that "the word State in our name is misleading," forewarns American employees and competitors alike that the Dutch government does not protect this enterprise from the chill winds that other businesses must face.

Other state multinationals contend that they are business corporations out to make a profit and contribute to the prosperity of their home countries through jobs at home and investments abroad. At first glance these statements seem to defy an exact translation into terms understood here. To say "We should invest in the United States," as they do, is difficult for us to accept, because in our whole range of post-Civil War economic experience we have denigrated government as enterprise banker, owner, and manager. Yet these multinationals have shown that they are here to stay, combining ties to Old World governments and relationships with American chambers of commerce.

Where To Begin

Most members of the management team employed in the host country should be local people who went to school and have business experience with local bankers, brokers, and government officials. Perhaps the chief financial officer can come from the home country; others may rotate through the local subsidiary, training for more responsibility. Critical ties between home and host countries must be maintained.

The top executive of the local subsidiary must understand his total corporate profile. If he is to translate foreign corporate goals and help the parent firm meet both business and social goals, then he must make state enterprise capitalism work in the host country under current customs and legislation.

The commercial decisions of state enterprise managers are influenced, for better or worse, by the economic policies of their home governments. The objectives of economic expansion must be incorporated into the strategies for building up or phasing down production and marketing systems of the world enterprise. We can note that Norsk Hydro was brought back under closer home government supervision because government insisted on investing more heavily in the Norwegian sector of the North Sea. Norsk Hydro management had to ask itself difficult questions about investments and divestments. Should it continue its petrochemical expansion and bauxite joint-venture investment in Norway? Should it go ahead with its ammonia investment in Scotland and its fertilizer investment in Qatar? It decided to maintain these investments and abandon its petroleum exploration investment in Colorado. Facing its $3 million loss on twenty-six dry holes, management yielded to Norwegian government pressure.

Divestment—a business decision influenced by the home government—should be part of the state firm's long-term strategic plan. VW sold off its Australian subsidiary, has refused to put new money into its South African subsidiary, and has decided to accept government partnership in its Mexican subsidiary.[3] All three are no-growth, no-profit situations. By divesting VW can use new capital to build up its American, Brazilian, and German subsidiaries.

The decision to invest overseas continues to be risky. In 1965, the German aluminum state enterprise, Vaw, bought the Channel Master Corporation of Ellenville, New York, with its 35,000-ton mill and facilities to make aluminum tubes.[4] This decision, a sound one at the time, failed to expand Vaw's international role. Vaw's place in the American market is not static. Vaw has no additional plants and subsidiaries, does not use its subsidiary as an export base for Latin America, and fails to take full advantage of its location in North America. Twelve years ago Vaw could have been the first to play the new game of building up an American subsidiary, but it failed to expand as fast as the market for aluminum tubes. Marginal in its market, it became vulnerable to being cut off as a supplier. Now, buyers do not want to carry Vaw products as inventory because Vaw can no longer provide proper marketing services.

Vaw management failed to analyze properly what its customers expected of it. While the enterprise acquired a sound business, management failed to understand the scale required to compete successfully. Vaw had no marketing strategy.

Giving a state enterprise that perfect-sized market overseas is always difficult. Management must make sound decisions about business needs, as well as about the ambitions of the host government. CFP, which has the reputation of an aggressive marketer in Great Britain, doubled its distribution capacity there by taking over the Arco retail marketing system.[5] Knowing what its business objectives should be, Elf-Aquitaine converted the discount operations of Occidental Petroleum to full-size gasoline stations.[6] Together, both French state multinationals have sufficient market size in Britain that they can earn the higher yields there which are denied them in France.

An essential step toward competitive strength is their ability to join forces when exploring for oil in the North Sea, thereby spreading the high risks between them. When new markets are opened up, they go their separate ways in setting up retail marketing systems. Yet they still help each other when they can. For example, all Renault cars exported to Britain will provide their purchasers with the information that Elf oil products are the manufacturer's recommended products.[7] Such tie-in arrangements, common among French enterprises, can be expected to increase in the United States in both the exploration and marketing of petroleum.

The American subsidiary is crucial to the state multinational. To achieve world-wide results, it is necessary to compete here. Not to do so might endanger the enterprise. Not to be here reduces chances of learning the newer marketing techniques that come from the American market. Not to be here first and with the proper resources means the state enterprise will have to catch up with other foreign firms, as Renault is now doing with VW, or be pushed aside as other firms dominate the market. For Norsk Hydro, which abandoned the market altogether, it means continuing only as a potential multinational for years to come.

Investments overseas demand new organizational structures. The question "Should we invest in the United States?" means managers must redesign their headquarters operations. Such reorganization is always fraught with new dangers and shunned by all but the most determined executives. At best, it takes several years for the state enterprise to shake down a new organizational structure so that it makes sense, does what it is supposed to do, and helps the enterprise meet its goals.

DSM, for instance, modified its corporate structure as it moved from being a domestic coal state enterprise, to a chemical state enterprise engaged in international business, and then to a petrochemical state multinational enterprise. Its current template places Nipro, Inc., the caprolactam subsidiary, and Columbia Nitrogen Corporation, the fertilizer subsidiary (both of Augusta, Georgia) under the Chemical Products Division headquartered in Limburg, The Netherlands.[8]

The American subsidiary's effective activities have been directed toward taking over a larger share of the raw materials market for nylon with caprolactam. This success helped management convince the parent organization to double Nipro's annual capacity. And when Nypro Ltd. of Flixborough, England was destroyed, American caprolactam capacity helped DSM even-out distribution problems.

Polysar's strategy for building up market position in America is essentially by acquisition. Polysar Latex (Chattanooga) is its only grass-roots factory; it was built from scratch, specifically to produce technologically superior rubber backing and underlay near its customers, the carpet manufacturers of Dalton, Georgia. All seven of Polysar's other plants were acquired.[9] Polysar managers knew that their new technology could revolutionize the industry if produced and marketed successfully, but Polysar had to suffer through the stage of its Chattanooga plant being "the wrong size" until its sales and distribution system caught up with production capacity. The team was never sure it would succeed; about two-thirds of all grass-roots developments fail in American markets.

Both the grass-roots plant and the seven acquisitions share the strategy to build an American rubber-mixing business with economies of scale for the entire North American market. Polysar has contributed substantially to each of its acquisitions by raising capacity and improving results. Before acquisition, the firms were too small to raise capital, too small to have research and development capability, and too small to negotiate prices from the auto firms. The "Big Three" were questioning the ability to supply quantities of products on time. After acquisition, they were part of a $400 million international firm with good research and development and with the power of the Canadian government behind it to force the auto firms to pay for their products.

Better Management Utilization of Distribution System

A decade before Polysar chose to focus on synthetic rubber products, Veba's Stinnes subsidiary decided to concentrate on machine tools, buying American Drill Brushing Co. and Richard Brothers Punch in the early 1960s.[10] Until the mid-1970s, Stinnes paid little attention to its other American businesses and did not aggressively compete for rebuilding locomotives. Then in 1974 its subsidiary, Precision National Leasing Corporation, bought eighty diesel locomotives from the Rock Island Line, reconditioned them, and leased them back.[11] Stinnes also continues in machine tools. Recently, it decided that its survival depended on increasing the scale of its export distribution system. The company decided to manage Youngstown Sheet and Tube's steel exports in Latin America and the eastern hemisphere.[12]

But how many state enterprise executives realize that their firm's growth, perhaps its long-term survival in the United States and other developed countries, depends on development of new products, new ways of distribution, and new organizational structures? Amid concern that these American subsidiaries may ossify as Vaw did, the emphasis is on marketing innovation.

Continued world-wide maturation is inherent in business firms, and government-owned and -supported enterprises are no exception. An American base is an important condition to improved profitability. Such investment increases market penetration, improves the export situation, and creates more subsidiaries overseas. It forces state enterprises to organize to use scarce resources as productively as possible so as not to flounder at home, in the United States, or in Third World markets.

Semiautonomous Management Teams

One characteristic of all multinationals (state, government-supported, or private) is that they require several top management teams. Each must recognize which team has primary responsibility in what geographical, functional, and production and marketing system area, and with what limitations. Yet this diversity must be harmonized. For BP and Sohio, fundamental unity comes from the enterprise's desire to link its Alaskan oil with an established Midwest marketing system. A common production and marketing system makes this unification successful.

BP's top management oversees the flow of funds to build the Alaskan pipeline, constructing the pipeline, and maintaining BP's working relationships with federal, state, and local governments. BP's management teams plan for the use of dividend income in the North Sea oil and Australian coal projects. Sohio's management works on building transportation, storage, and refining facilities for Alaskan oil; on arranging a new series of oil swap arrangements between itself (now as a West Coast importer) and East Coast importers; and on building a better, more integrated retail marketing system from the former BP and Sohio gasoline stations on the eastern seaboard and in the Midwest.

Parent Enterprise Decides on
Overall Corporate Strategy

There is a caveat to the independence of the local subsidiary. The top management of the parent enterprise—not that of the local subsidiary—makes decisions on overall strategy. The parent firm must decide; otherwise there is disunity.

There are three basic risks in permitting two or more top managements to operate: (1) it becomes difficult to assign work clearly among teams; (2) the work must fit a total geographical, functional, and production and marketing system of the parent company and also fit local subsidiary goals; and (3) there must be rules for which team is to be given most support and when these relationships can change because of the new needs, products, and markets facing the world enterprise. Let's look at some of the more successful efforts.

Good industrial market research told DSM that Latin American caprolactam export sales would improve if the firm followed the normal, post-Second World War habit and supported its American subsidiary as the major export base. Latin American industrial customers were accustomed to buying many new, technically superior products from American firms and considered most European companies somewhat behind in providing new, world-scale technologies. By examining its distribution system, Stinnes found it had excess capital and marketing talent in its American subsidiary and permitted its local management team to export steel products for a privately-owned American firm.

These divisions of responsibilities worked well because all top management agreed with the parent enterprise's overall business strategies. Such an effort could not work without agreement on how to determine which subsidiary can do the job best, who will decide, and how it can be done with the least disruption among competing subsidiaries.

What distinguishes the state multinational from privately-owned international firms is that it creates unity of purpose, strategy, and tasks among its diverse personnel while at the same time being committed to a particular nation-state. It becomes both a business firm and a publicly-recognized representative of a foreign government. Yet local subsidiaries are dependent upon one another. What each does affcts the other, and there can be management problems. When DSM builds a caprolactam plant in Britain, the export sales of its American subsidiary, Nipro, suffer. When the English subsidiary, Nypro, is forced to close its operations, the United States subsidiary must sell caprolactam to it at cost, losing its mark-up and its goodwill among its own American buyers and Latin American customers. Why is the English subsidiary considered a preferred customer? And will this transaction force the United States Internal Revenue Service to reconstruct Nipro's accounts, insist on an "arms-length" exchange, and charge it the penalties due under Section 482 of the IRS code?

When the 1973 oil crisis began, BP claimed that it was bound by its parent relationship to supply Sohio with as much crude as possible, even diverting its supply from traditional affiliates in Western Europe and Asia.[13] This saved Sohio's retail system but angered the French and the Japanese. To make matters worse, United States authorities raised questions about whether Sohio was paying the market price or whether the crude was too high so as to insure higher taxes paid to Great Britain.

Whether state multinationals will succeed or fail in the United States depends upon their ability to resolve complex business problems within a cultural setting and governmental context far different from those in their home countries. To be successful, the parent enterprise's top management team has to permit its subsidiary's top management team to carry out its work in a way compatible with American values, habits, and customs.

Nexus Stability

A stable nexus is crucial to success of state enterprise investments in the United States as well as those elsewhere. New market thrusts especially must be acceptable to the home government. If it has not consented to export of capital and the production and marketing system, it might repudiate the investment. Such a mistake is contrary to the tie that binds a state enterprise to a government.

Several examples show how stable relationships permeate state enterprise business activities at home, in the United States and elsewhere, and how remote is the notion that state enterprises will assume tasks that run counter to the long-term interests of their home governments. Yet stability does little to provide profit unless the investments are managed successfully. Both competitive position and economic performance are jeopardized when state enterprise executives do not manage foreign investment properly.

Network of Contacts

State enterprise management in the United States is a large and rapidly growing—yet unnoticed—network of top executives, financial accountants, market researchers, detail salesmen, engineers, foremen, billing clerks, and factory workers. It embraces the American offices of the home government's industrial planning ministeries, e.g., the French Industrial Planning Agency and their congeries of American-based chambers of commerce. It can call upon a huge financial network, a vast communication system, a great array of distribution institutions, and numerous specialized consulting and legal organizations, making state enterprises capable of major new investments.

The key to successful management in the United States is the ability to raise capital in Wall Street, to gain good advertising services from Madison Avenue, and to have expert legal advice when seeking to take over additional American firms in the face of the antitrust laws. If these services are effectively tied-in, then state enterprises will have the means to compete here. Although the financial and marketing connections may differ from country to country, the need to establish such a network is the same for all enterprises making foreign direct investments.

Entrepreneurial Tasks

Whatever an enterprise's set of foreign direct investments, its management must follow four basic rules for success: it must (1) take on all the entrepreneurial tasks; (2) make purposeful investments; (3) increase market share and maintain market control; and (4) nourish the nexus.

The effective management of direct investments embraces all the entrepreneurial tasks. For instance, a petroleum state enterprise must find new sources of crude. It must have on its staff geologists and others who can read satellite maps of rock formations and who can pinpoint the probable location of oil. But management must also have the talent needed to capitalize a pipeline, bulkhead terminals, a tanker fleet, refineries, and a retail marketing system. Entrepreneurial performance requires management not only to make important new discoveries but also to make them available through world-scale production and marketing systems.

The Better Investment

An American investment's capital needs can be greater than comparable investments elsewhere, for our market is much larger and diverse. Demanding extensive use of sophisticated technologies and complex marketing services dwarfing those elsewhere, an American subsidiary can insatiably devour capital. As a result, marginal investments in South Africa, Asia, and Australia are starved for funds.

American investments claim priority because most of them serve important nexus goals. They provide both the state enterprise and the home government with security of raw materials and repatriated dividends, the opportunity to learn how to compete in a continental-size market, and the prospect for reducing multinational competition back home. As American investments grow, they come to be more than just another foreign direct investment of a state enterprise. They serve as the essential link to world-scale production, the critical barometer of an enterprise's fortunes, and as the refuge from the socio-political problems facing entrepreneurial risk-taking and managerial performance in many areas of the world.

The effective management of an American investment consists of several essential tasks: (1) setting up a subsidiary whose organizational structure fits the character of the domestic market but which can link itself closely and smoothly to the foreign parent enterprise; (2) devising strategies for creating sources of capital, raw materials, distribution channels, and executive talent in supply markets; and (3) positioning products and their sales promotion campaigns in end-use markets. When completed successfully here, they outshine anything that can be achieved elsewhere. Thus additional investments are being made in the United States by state enterprises at the expense of other areas of the world.

The Money-making Investment

If it is presumed that the American subsidiary is a "money-making machine," the conclusion must then be that additional investment in sources of raw materials, product design, marketing connections, promotional expenses, and line and staff organization will further parent enterprise interests. Since state enterprises invest to build up market share, an additional set of foreign government-owned firms actively participate in the American market. To curb them would curtail this competitive struggle, reducing benefits from lower prices, better services, or both.

Such a notion fails to take into account that state enterprises offer their products in highly-specialized market segments. When the VW Beetle was price-competitive, no combination of new models, advertising slogans, and price discounts could shake the loyalty of VW Beetle owners. Brand loyalty to an inexpensive and efficient means of transportation permitted VW to monopolize this market segment, fully employ its German and Brazilian workers, and prosper as no other foreign automobile firm has done before or after in the United States.

The present disposition of the American business community to encourage market control by state enterprises is inappropriate. It may be fine for consumer goods such as

Elf-Aquitaine's health and personal care items. No purpose is served by challenging its investment in Towne, Paulsen, & Co.[14] Nor will the discovery that direct investments in America have an organic role in the economic prosperity of other nation-states seem important. Yet the general effect of these foreign direct investments is to transfer control over resources and manufacturing firms to foreign government interests, where they are beyond our control.

This control is becoming absolute. The specific strategy consists first in finding a candidate for takeover—an acquisition of a wholly-owned or joint-venture subsidiary. To the extent it succeeds, it means that the parent has an established vehicle for pouring in its capital funds and managerial talent. The state enterprise then joins with other firms to develop a reasonable division of its market. There is a crude equilibrium process at work which gives each participating firm an appropriate share of the market. As the case of Vaw showed, the state enterprise must have the resources to play the game. It must be able to bear the huge costs of expanding volume to meet the growth its share of the market enjoys, or it will fall by the wayside.

Given the goals of the state enterprise and its home government, those enterprises with large reserves of raw materials (BP), unique technologies (Polysar and DSM), and capability for price discrimination (VW) will seek to upset this equilibrium. As their market share expands at the expense of domestic competition, they will dominate the market, reinforced by sales and advertising strategies, new products and models, better inventory and cash flow management, and periodic infusion of new capital.

The management of foreign direct investments is in all respects an admirably subtle arrangement in linking the nexus to the host country market. It convinces Americans they are purchasing goods from just another business firm. No case for foreign government intervention in the domestic market seems possible.

The consequence: while government-owned and -supported enterprises become more important in the American market, their governments are not seen to have any influence here at all. On the contrary, it requires an act of will to imagine any connection between business success here and prosperity back in the home country. Emotionally, we agree that federal and state governments should not intervene in the economy. But in fact we have failed to note how state enterprises have brought such foreign government intervention in our domestic market economy.

Since sales growth, market position, and profits are hallmarks of success for industrial firms, the enviable results of this managerial effort by government-owned firms enhances the prestige of the state enterprise capitalism system. State enterprise managers have refuted the axiom that state-owned firms will bungle efforts to make pricing decisions over investments, supplies and equipment, and labor.

State enterprises are willing to pay the market price or better for their acquisitions, inducing American businessmen to sell out for a lifetime annuity for themselves and their friends. They reject federal dictates on who can buy the manufacturing firm as government interference in the free enterprise system. The problem is not one of original error but of obsolescence. The notion of businessmen being free to decide the buyers and prices of their businesses was appropriate when the buyers were privately-owned multinationals. At that time, which was another era in international business, home government influence on the foreign investment decisions of businessmen was weak, and thus commercial acquisitions had neutral impact upon the strength of foreign governments. This model was not wrong for those conditions. The error is in applying it without change in the emerging era, where it does not correspond to the new realities of the world's political economy.

The temptation is to be unconcerned about acquisitions of American firms because most have been small-scale. The common tendency throughout the American business community to misunderstand what is happening is just as common in government. The private-firm manager tells the State Department it should buy potash from the Soviet Union rather than from the state enterprises of Saskatchewan, France, and Morocco because the Soviet Union is a more secure supplier.[15] The argument that a socialist country from Eastern Europe is a more secure supplier than two of our Western allies is simply not valid, but its advocacy by those who should know better makes it difficult to develop a rational policy towards foreign state multinational enterprises.

Some eleven state and twenty government-supported firms have investments here with more than four times that many in the wings. More than half of these potential investors have the capacity to make the organizational changes necessary to bring success to their American investments. Most European and Japanese government-subsidized enterprises are especially ready to invest, and the Brazilians cannot be far behind. Vale do Rio Doce has already bought a coal mine in British Columbia to furnish coal for its growing steel industry in Minas Gerais, Brazil. The United States also could provide the same resource to enable Brazil to manufacture even more steel.

The axiom of traditional investment theory is that state enterprises support the domestic and foreign economic policies of their home governments. In fact, whatever state enterprises do for their commercial investments and whatever state enterprise managers do to create profitable production and marketing systems at home and abroad is for the good of their home governments.

Foreign direct investment is a problem of organization. The proper rule for state enterprise managers today is to view their organizations, strategies, and assignments as transitory, subject to alteration as products and markets change their demands on management's time and as the nexus assigns new tasks. Great state enterprise managers will make the American market accommodate itself to these new economic demands of foreign governments.

13

Economic Power and Business Management

ALL OF the successful state enterprise managers, from Elf-Aquitaine's Pierre Guillaumat to CDC's H. Anthony Hampson, decided purposefully to invest in the United States. Hampson, for example, has always understood correctly that his enterprise has both business and socioeconomic goals. He convinced wary governments and unions that their best interests lie in expanding to another country. He persuaded them to accept his definition of the enterprise's mission. He shaped the discussion around how the firm will help the home national economy while making profits critical to the firm's long-term prosperity.

Only a clear sense of mission makes a clear international business objective possible. It is the foundation for exporting production and marketing systems. It is the beginning for assessing American trade restrictions versus the cost and revenue streams in the American market. It defines the purpose of business and provides the rationale for foreign direct investments.

The Opportune Decision

The success of VW resulted from a new corporate strategy created when the enterprise needed markets overseas to counter the rebirth of GM and Ford in Germany. When Heinz Nordhoff became chief executive officer immediately after the Second World War, the VW plant and organization was in ruins. Nordhoff forced his company to begin exporting to The Netherlands in 1947 and to the United States soon thereafter to earn hard currency for rebuilding Germany's shattered economy. By developing a mass marketing strategy for Germany, Italy, and Norway, and by diversifying in many markets without adding an expensive multiplicity of products, he enabled VW to dominate many export markets, including the American foreign car market.

VW made its Brazilian foreign direct investment in 1955, just about the time the "Big Three" American auto manufacturers made major investments in Western Europe. By the early 1960s, the enterprise was the major producer of cars in Brazil and a major exporter of cars to the United States. It foresaw the need to become an investor in the United States early in the 1970s, when unfavorable changes in exchange rates, increased shipping costs, and higher German wage rates were hiking the cost of VWs in America. The German federal government agreed, but the German unions and the government of Lower Saxony did not. During this difficult period, VW's market share of all cars sold in the American market dropped from 6.1 to 3.3 percent,[1] profits declined, and VW began to incur losses. Only in 1976 did the unions reluctantly agree to VW manufacturing its cars in New Stanton, Pennsylvania.

The VW story reaffirms the central importance of giving state enterprise managers a free hand in deciding corporate mission and purpose. Yet it also shows that this alone is not enough. The manager must be able to follow through unimpeded by fears of unions and government, otherwise market timing for foreign direct investment fails.

Market timing is crucial. Cost and revenue streams may change because of new tariffs, new currency rates, or a host of other reasons. As early as 1969, VW had difficulties maintaining its volume of exports to the United States. One-quarter of its world production, 500,000 units, were sold here annually.[2] VW's more expensive cars, the product of mergers with Auto Union and NSU, did not sell well in the United States as American owners of the Beetle traded up to other more expensive foreign and domestic cars. VW's line of cars was so uncoordinated that their proliferation threatened the economies of scale key to the Beetle's success. This realization forced Kurt Lotz out as chairman in 1971. His successor, Rudolph Leiding, corrected these mistakes, increased capital outlays substantially at a time when unit sales were down, and pushed for the same American investment his predecessor wanted. He too was forced out in 1974 because he insisted on this foreign direct investment.

VW was perceived as a German firm. Toni Schmuecker, the new chairman, and his management team realized that to change this image, they had to sell the unions and the public on how an American investment could improve the German economy—indeed, that the American market was indispensable to the success of the German firm. This required radical innovations in building public support: constant indoctrination in the wisdom of this investment for Germany, for the unions, and for VW; and emphasis on taking care of all potential labor-redundancy problems. It meant a policy on factory closings which assumed that the company would help the local German community affected and that top management would find new jobs for laid-off employees and new industry for the community losing its factory. VW could not have committed $200 million to its Pennsylvania plant without this careful cultivation of its publics.

The Emden factory in Lower Saxony produces 60 percent of all Golfs and is in a high-unemployment area. Schmuecker himself assured the Emden works council that there would be no further loss of jobs when the production of Golfs (Rabbits) was shifted to New Stanton. He also assured the governments of Lower Saxony and at Bonn that without a plant in the United States, VW's market share of imported cars would drop to such an extent that it could never be regained. He was a true diplomat in bringing all German parties to agree on the wisdom of the investment.

Schmuecker's actions took nearly two years to work out. Each was considered un-German when first proposed and was bitterly resisted by the communities and unions. Schmuecker dared hire a GM executive, McLernon, to get Rabbits rolling from the New Stanton plant, first in an assembly operation, and then in a fully-integrated manufacturing business. One way to tell whether a particular state enterprise top manager is able to follow through on his plans is to see whom he hires and what responsibilities he gives them.

The building of these American subsidiaries during the last fifteen years is primarily the work of a small number of great state enterprise managers. These men all had one common insight and one common objective. The domestic state enterprise had become obsolete, sterile, and unproductive. The managers wanted to establish state enterprises fully competitive with firms in the private sector and realized that although American and Swiss examples had much to offer, state multinational enterprises had to be public-sector firms.

Beyond these shared beliefs, however, they differed sharply on business strategies for building up their American subsidiaries. BP's Sir Eric Drake saw the purpose of acquiring Sohio in making Royal Dutch Shell realize that the latter had a European government firm which now could compete all over the world. Ian Rush at Polysar, Hans Schudel at Stinnes, and W. A. J. Bogers at DSM saw the development of the American subsidiary as the creation of a new order based upon the combination of American managerial practice and European ordering. Their companies had to be important internationals in their own right rather than off-shoots of another time and place in history. René Granier de Lilliac of CFP and Pierre Guillaumat of Elf-Aquitaine saw the American subsidiary as the fulfillment of their country's hopes and expectations.

Each knew how to satisfy their multiple constituencies— home government, host government, private bankers, suppliers, unions, and customers. Most had to build their new state enterprises on old foundations but had to satisfy their new capital needs and new market demands almost immediately after making the commitment to become competitive internationally. They were all exceedingly conscious of the need to attract and hold financial support from their international bankers.

Each of these men gave priority to applying proven business strategies to their new market. Some were very successful, while others were not. Even during their tenure they saw their state enterprises become whole new beings, throw off the rigidities of domestic state enterprises, and become more like their competition, the international business firm.

In 1960, state enterprise capitalism did not exist in America. By 1977, state multinational enterprises had become established as competitors in a wide range of markets. Their domestic subsidiaries had a distinctly American cast no matter how some of their exiled executives sighed for Parisian cuisine.

PART FIVE

American Decisions

14

Reciprocity

THE SPECIAL NETWORK of contacts for state enterprise investment is gradually binding American manufacturing firms, financial institutions, advertising agencies, and law firms to foreign national planning ministries. Cutting across ideological lines, it contains Canadian nationalists, British socialists, French statists, German capitalists, Russian communists, and Brazilian militarists. It could serve as a "new world economic order." Its policy about government intervention in the economy is clear: direct investment in the United States is appropriate as long as it serves the best interests of the home country. Most want resources and dividends from America, and what is good for them may not be equally good for us.

An effective policy of reciprocity requires a common understanding of what is appropriate investment strategy in both countries. Although now applicable only to leaseholdings on federal lands, reciprocity is the right rule for us to insist upon. By and large, its imperatives do not conflict with the traditions of workable competition among American firms.

The Lessons We Need to Learn

Foreign government intervention by means of state enterprise direct investment has produced a profound change in our ties to the international economy. None of the free-market safeguards we favor has been able to withstand the pressures of state enterprise capitalism. It has changed the face of competition among nations.

When state enterprises were first introduced sixty years ago in response to domestic economic problems, no businessman saw the shift in the international business center of gravity, much less the need for a host country policy to limit the direct investments. One government's solution to its foreign economic relations became another's problem; the nexus was in conflict.

The most effective nexuses tailored their external economic policies for the greatest gains socially, economically, and politically. For instance, they offered joint business arrangements to Third World countries without accommodating the United States. Wholly-owned American subsidiaries are very important to the performance of state multinationals, and it is obvious that the nexuses will fight a long and hard battle to maintain their positions here. Had we understood what these state enterprises were, what their home governments permitted our firms to do, and what the alternative policies could be, we might now have a more favorable relationship to these foreign nexuses. We could have avoided having our resources alienated, or at least could have channelled them for American use.

The first lesson is to recognize that state enterprise capitalism can be used in resolving critical domestic policies. For example, neither privately-owned energy firms nor foreign petroleum state enterprises can resolve America's energy problem collectively because they can't handle the enormous capital costs of new technology. It is tempting to threaten to break their integrated operations into constituent parts as if this will "solve" the energy problems, but such a policy might even do serious damage to the existing energy industry.

Surely, if state enterprise success teaches us anything, it is that the energy crisis would best be handled by some form of national economic planning. This would force American-based energy firms to concentrate on resolving the problems of highest priority. In the short run, this would include better management of supply; in the longer run, this must be development of new technologies. The federal government would contribute its capital to the latter. We must insist that both the government and business work together to resolve the energy problem.

There is another important lesson: to understand that state enterprise capitalism has influence upon America's external relations. In the mid-1970s it is clear that the United States must depend economically upon foreign state enterprise capitalism. We need to collaborate with some and compete against other nexuses. In the next decade, this dependency will deepen. To manage supply of resources, the government must work with business firms to provide the nation with an equitable distribution of oil, coal, phosphate, and other important commodities. Of all the lessons of state enterprise capitalism and the international business change underlying it, this necessary relationship between government and business will be the hardest one to accept.

This leads us to the issues of reciprocity which underlie our economic relations with foreign nexuses, especially the ownership share the foreign investor is permitted in the local firm. For example, American firms are not allowed to buy British coal mines. Yet British firms are allowed to buy American coal mines. Equality of treatment under a policy of reciprocity is absent where the home government works with its state and government-supported enterprises to exclude or limit the participation of American firms in the domestic economy.

Other limitations on American firms illustrate lopsided foreign economic relations. (1) Production-sharing agreements in the petroleum industry give American firms only a minority share of their total liftings for downstream activities; the majority share goes to the home petroleum state enterprise "partner" for distribution through its own marketing system. (2) Market-sharing agreements give American firms only a percentage of the national market, while the majority portion of the market is reserved for home firms. (3) Government-owned and -supported enterprises are given special subsidies in the form of tax incentives, low cost loans, and nonpayment of social security expenses, which are available to private firms only as partners of state enterprises. (4) Foreign investment codes preclude American firms from certain resource-related investments. (5) Investment capital is not made available to American firms because they are not included within the five-year forecasts of national economic plans. Each home government-state enterprise nexus has special rules restricting the commercial behavior of American multinationals.

Magnitude of the Problem

This unequal treatment has had consequences whose large significance is beginning to become distinct. By the close of 1977, over $1 billion of direct investments by state enterprises revealed only a portion of the massive phenomenon: many investments for undisclosed amounts; ten times that amount of direct investments by privately-owned firms, whose policies are controlled in large part by their home governments; the costs of cartelized world production, which mean higher oil prices, larger balance of payments deficits, plus dumped stainless steel and resulting increased unemployment; and costs associated with unavailability of resources because they are shipped to foreign markets by state enterprises that own American oil, coal, and phosphate.

The specific impact of state enterprise capitalism upon the United States comes to $50 billion—three percent of the GNP. Yet the full impact—trade restrictions, foreign investment controls, market- and production-sharing agreements, and special tax benefits—is just not known.

We do know that the state enterprise share of the world economy will grow and prosper, while the private-firm share will decline. Without any provision for the expansion of state enterprise capitalism, our foreign economic policies enable state enterprises to use their advantages to gain access to and control of our markets.

Need for Reciprocity

Privately-owned American firms no longer have easy access to foreign national economies and their raw materials and manufacturing facilities. Instead, commercial ventures with equity ties to home governments are preferred, and American firms are required to provide capital, technology, and marketing connections for only a limited-ownership position.

When our firms refuse to accept these conditions, they are frozen out of markets. For example, after Brazil set up government-subsidized enterprises to build a domestic computer industry, it required foreign investors, such as IBM, to provide technology and guaranteed the sales of domestic firms to other Brazilian state enterprises. American firms refused to debundle their technology and marketing services. The Japanese did not. The same semiconductor and computer firms that the Japanese government is financing to oust American firms from market dominance—Fujitsu, Hitachi, Sharp, and Cannon—are providing their Brazilian partners (Electrônica Digital, Computadores Sistemas Brasileiros, Labo Electrônica, and Sharp Equipamentos) with entry-level technology. Brazilian marketing restrictions tied in with Japanese strategy to capitalize on our own discomfort seriously impair the ability of American firms to compete in the world economy.

The rapid expansion of the number of state enterprises and of their sales and asset positions coincides with the emergence of a militant drive for equality between developed and Third World nations. Gifts and loans of capital, manufacturing processes, and marketing services become the driving passion of less-developed nations. There is no explicit federal government program to provide tax relief or other forms of compensation when an American firm must sell its newly-developed technology without maintaining managerial control through a wholly-owned subsidiary. Privately-owned firms that have no ties to their home governments, such as American firms, are at an increasing disadvantage compared with all other Canadian, European, Japanese, and Third World firms in the emerging world economic order.

The standard prescription for overcoming this disadvantage is to request federal government action to negotiate a reduction in tariff and nontariff barriers under the General Agreement on Tariffs and Trade. If only these preferential treatments were eliminated, then equal access to foreign markets would be assured. This is what international trade theorists meant by free trade. But removing the barriers to movements of goods does nothing about the unequal amounts of government subsidies in local capital and labor markets. These distort economic performance and make some trade and investment decisions more profitable than others. Nor does removing these barriers address issues of the unequal share interests governments hold in state enterprises and the unequal financial controls governments insist upon over so-called private firms. These are the motors behind rationalization programs. It is this approach to state enterprise capitalism that has been in the ascent these last decades.

State enterprise capitalism means marshalling all the nation-state's resources and the talent to enable the nation-state to compete better in the world market. We therefore have to develop an approach towards making the United

States more comfortable with the evolving economic order. There is no best solution in sight. The policy of bilateral reciprocity is how compromises between two nexuses can be made. The real question is whether the United States is willing to organize itself to make this policy work.

For example, the Bank of Japan and the Ministry of Finance maintain tight control over American banks in Japan—a very subtle form of protectionism. Our branches cannot seek savings deposits, issue debentures, or incorporate there. The government limits their ability to bring in foreign exchange, make currency swaps, and gives them low quotas on loans. Japanese banks in America have no such restrictions placed on them by the Comptroller of the Currency or the Federal Reserve. They have freedom that their American counterparts lack. To force them into reciprocal treatment we would have to encourage our several bank regulatory authorities to apply the same "administrative guidance" to their branches as they do to ours.

Should we instruct our federal agencies to apply similar "administrative guidance" to other situations demanding reciprocity? We say yes.

What did we lose—and France gain—when Honeywell sold its majority interest in CII-Honeywell Bull to the French government and local private interests? Exports of American-made large and minicomputers are reduced as production of these is shifted to France, and jobs and the tax base that go with them are gone. And this is not all. The local firm received $250 million in government grants and $800 million in orders from the French government. This is a significant financial tie to commit the firm to its new course—as a French government-supported private firm —subsidized by France, but built on American technology.

How many more of these valuable resources can we afford to lose? Not many.

We see France going after our main-frame technology and Japan after our minicomputer technology. Brazil wants in, too. Where does it end before we develop a comprehensive reciprocity policy?

In a decade, will we be faced with the situation we now have in steel? Europe competes with us in basic steel technology. Japan helps Third World countries build their steel industry so that neither American nor European steel products are welcome in Brazil, Taiwan, or South Korea. And Japan itself shifts to higher-technology items that are big sellers in the United States. Our response is to limit their exports to us rather than forcing them to open their domestic distribution systems to our products. The impact upon our domestic market could be pernicious—more costly and technologically inferior products sold to American customers. Wouldn't it be better to declare them not in reciprocal status with us and prohibit their products from our markets until a comprehensive understanding can be negotiated through diplomatic channels?

Any foreign restrictions on the production and sale of our goods and services—whether these be regulations on bank loans, prohibitions on domestic monopolies from buying foreign goods, or requirements to shift manufacturing operations overseas—should be met in kind. There should be an attorney general's ruling declaring their firms ineligible to invest, produce, and distribute in our domestic market. The simplicity of the strategy outweighs all the elegant arguments raised by the Department of State for a policy of leniency against foreign cartels, nexuses, and state- and government-supported enterprises.

When we see how crucial certain foreign acts are to our fate, we move speedily to put into place a bilateral reciprocal policy. In 1977, we entered into such an agreement with Saudi Arabia. We provide them with $20.9 billion in nonmarketable government securities—a new set of "Roosa" bonds—in return for oil (to build up our strategic petroleum reserve), military hardware, and development assistance. This sale of "twilight paper" is equivalent to a bilateral loan by Saudi Arabia to the United States—but one that can't be called before the maturity date, some two to seven years hence. The Treasury takes care of the sale of these government securities, the "Fed" adds them to its portfolio of funds managed for the Saudi central bank, and the Defense Department arranges for the sale of airplanes and missiles. This constitutes a coordinated government program, under the overall foreign-policy guidance of the State Department, to insure that America gets its oil while at the same time neutralizing America's IOUs and preventing these new "dollars" from crossing the foreign exchanges.

The real question is whether the United States is willing to organize itself to make reciprocity work in banking, petroleum, mining, steel, computers, and other sectors of the international economy.

15

Orderly Marketing Agreements

STATE ENTERPRISE CAPITALISM should not be regarded as something apart from national governments.
Rather, it should be seen as the vehicle for present-day
international economic relations among nation-states. All
state enterprises are subordinate to their home governments; their managers derive authority from working within
the nexus. This fully allows them to work in association with
government ministers and private industrialists, both domestic and foreign, and to accomplish the commercial tasks
that the government bureaucracy cannot do for itself. Tasks
of national economic planning fuse state enterprise management, state enterprises, state enterprise capitalism, and
the nation-state. Americans will gradually recognize that
the American economy has already developed some habits
of state enterprise capitalism by necessity to deal with the

economic problems facing the nation, their huge capital cost requirements, and the decision to force the national economy to deliver results it would not produce if left to itself.

Such ties are not unusual. For example, the government finances, owns, and manages Conrail and Amtrak. Defense contractors work closely with the federal military establishment in planning the development and manufacture of new weapons. The Department of Defense itself acts as the export agent, as it did in the sale of the General Dynamics F-16 fighter plane to the NATO countries and other Western allies.[1]

Government commercial initiative has taken place in the nuclear-power industry and will intensify in shale oil, coal gasification, nuclear fusion, and solar power developments. Government's willingness to take a risk is likely to occur throughout all phases of the energy industry, under the control of government-owned energy firms and through the management of executives, hired from privately-owned firms, who will become another set of American state enterprise executives. It is likely that the initiative for the expansion of energy and minerals supplies will pass to the federal government as it has in the railroad and defense industries.

Will American state enterprise capitalism copy the decline of British and Italian state enterprise capitalism or the success of French state enterprise capitalism?

If the commercial state enterprise is recognized as a critical part of state enterprise capitalism, it will be seen in the service of the social goals of the nation-state that sets it up. It can be supplied the initial capital to begin managing energy. It can be authorized to expand supplies from do-

mestic sources, go into joint ventures with foreign oil partners, and be the government's arm in state-to-state economic
relations. It can be commanded to override judgments of
the private sector as long as government is willing to subsidize the full costs of nationally important, noncommercial
investments. And by withdrawing the subsidy it can turn
these into commercial investments whenever market conditions warrant.

The defect in British state enterprise capitalism is that
government is unwilling to create the conditions for additional industrial investment, greater levels of employment,
and more production of marketable output; it prefers to
subsidize the ineffective industrial structure which exists in
the British economy. The defect in Italian state enterprise
capitalism is that government is refusing to pay in full for
the noncommercial investments it authorized in the Mezzogiorno. It tried to overcome the structural imbalances in
its two regional economies and failed.

In contrast, the strength of Swedish state enterprise capitalism is that it gets government either to pay the full costs
of noncommercial investments, or these are not made.
When state enterprises cannot find buyers for their output
they cease production, merge with private firms, or are reorganized into more efficient production and marketing
systems. The strength of French state enterprise capitalism
is in this willingness to rationalize industrial organization
for the manufacture and sale of world-scale technology at
competitive prices in the market sector.

Imagine applications to the United States. As the value
of government-owned, commercially-responsive enterprises
comes to be recognized, attention must focus on organizing
and managing production and marketing systems suitable

to a mixed economy. Those who have the foresight to accept state enterprise investment where it is needed, to see where the partnership of state and private capital can best be utilized, and to understand where private investment alone is not most effective will benefit from America's economic pluralism, which others are now capturing.

Chambers of commerce and individual businessmen will attest to most of the individual developments which are leading to a pluralistic, mixed American economy—to the establishment of industrial state enterprise capitalism. Both federal and state governments intervene to countermand decisions of the market. They seek to protect groups lacking market power, to set up nationally important industries, to force new societal values upon business.[2] They employ one out of every three workers directly or indirectly.[3] These are all accepted facts of life.

The federal government probably won't intervene in these ways and then leave command over international mineral sourcing, division of "world product," foreign direct investment, and other foreign economic policies to Japan and the European nations. If the relationship of the government to business has changed in the domestic economy, it must also change in the international economy. If this associates the American government inextricably with food exporters, commodity traders, energy suppliers, extractors of minerals, and producers of new research and development, the fact must be understood and used to America's best advantage.

It may be argued that the government has no business in developing new technologies, in manufacturing and marketing them in the economy, or in expanding supplies of food, energy, and other critically-needed products. This may be true in small businesses. However, as Eli Ginzburg pointed out in a recent issue of *Scientific American*, "Important as the private sector has been in stimulating the growth of the economy, there is no way to read our recent history without recognizing the strategic part government and nonprofit institutions have played in providing new entrepreneurial structures for meeting new needs and desires of the public."[4] He and W. W. Rostow agree that "the key task ahead is to bring about a massive increase in investment through the collaboration of the public and private sectors. A public role is inescapable because, for good or ill, governments here and abroad are inextricably involved in policy towards energy, agriculture, raw materials, the environment, research and development."[5]

Governments do rebuild railroads, establish a nuclear power industry, and invest in new energy technologies. For governments use their fifty-nine petroleum, minerals, and manufacturing state enterprises (and their 234 government-supported private firms) to gain competitive advantage over other nation-states in foreign economic relations. The notion of independence from government in the international economy is a fiction.

All of these industrial state enterprises are patrolling the world in search of the least expensive, most secure sources of food, energy, minerals, and other products. Since 1972, there has been a sharp increase in the price of basic commodities, energy, and raw materials—the long cycle of business called the Kondratieff wave.[6] No new frontiers which brought prices down in previous periods are now open for settlement; technological breakthroughs must come from research and development. Before man's ingenuity can rescue him with a new source of energy or food, governments and their enterprises will have to collaborate to claim for national use as many resources as a host country is willing to surrender.

This is more deeply characteristic of the international economy than we like to admit. The tendency of the federal government, business, labor, and the general public *not* to see this link between domestic abundance and foreign economic penetration is key to our argument for reciprocity.

Those who dislike the notion that the federal government intervene in foreign direct investments made by state enterprises in the United States will be tempted to label it small-scale, unimportant. This is a mistake. Once an investment is made we dare not take it over, command its local subsidiaries to act contrary to its home government-state enterprise nexus, or restrict its commercial dealings in ways that do not apply to all business firms, foreign and domestic, private and state-owned. To do so would cause a diplomatic controversy and place American firms overseas in hostage.

American firms should see the larger picture. BP's Alaskan oil, Veba's West Virginia coal, and CDC's North Carolina phosphates are all depletable American resources. They could be critical during the next twenty to twenty-five years, when there will be high prices for scarce raw materials. Control over them will determine which national economy expands, whose workers will be employed, and whether citizens, allies or socialist business acquaintances pay inflated prices for their use. Until new technology is brought to market we, like all others, must depend upon the existing physical stock of plant and equipment to get us through this 1972–92 Kondratieff price upswing. Thereafter, given the opening of new technological frontiers, another Kondratieff price downswing will take place as it did in the 1820s, 1870s, 1920s, and 1950s. Seen in this light, an American nexus emphasizing close collaboration between the federal government and business is inevitable.

Host Country Policies

An important question about a foreign direct investment is whether it serves the needs of the host country. As we have seen, the foreign nexus is able to export resources and repatriate dividends without challenge from the federal government. It requires no host country policies to maximize its advantage to the home country. On the other hand, there would be no foreign direct investment if national economic policy precluded foreign state enterprises from setting up wholly-owned subsidiaries altogether.

The prospects for foreign direct investment throughout the world are far from clear. When the Canadian government set up its Foreign Investment Review agency, Canada thought that American direct investment would continue to flow no matter what national economic plans were set. Canada was wrong. The American divestment in Canada is directly tied to the requirements for investment review, the purchase of American subsidiaries by CDC, and by provincial state enterprises and other governmental intervention policies. In this case, American firms will sacrifice Canada because they can increase investments in the United States and maintain some of their northern market through exports. As state enterprise capitalism evolves elsewhere and away from America, the investment strategy turns from wholly-owned subsidiaries to joint business arrangements with local government-controlled interests.

American businesses will enter joint ventures to make a foreign direct investment, but only when forced. Is this reluctance why we have no policy requiring American participation in foreign direct investment here?

This suggestion is a natural corollary of reciprocity: we would treat their firms no better than they treat ours. Foreign state enterprises would have to share with our firms the energy resources and minerals found within our territory. The American partner would usually be a privately-owned firm; however, a federal energy corporation set up to develop shale oil or for gasification of coal could be a partner of Norsk Hydro, Veba, BP, and Elf-Aquitaine.

Classical Blinders

Conservative business executives have given us an outmoded policy of foreign direct investment. They have not noticed that their successors, the state enterprise managers, were uniting ever more closely with their home governments in part to alienate American resources. These executives were also enthusiastically selling their businesses to foreign state enterprises—a classical response which has been and will continue to be detrimental to America's best interests.

But the problem is not the freedom of American businessmen to sell their firms to foreign state enterprises. The danger lies in subordination of American economics to foreign politics.

If we continue to let each nation form cartels, evade its share of the costs of the Kondratieff wave, and enjoy protectionism, then the whole structure of world commerce could tumble. The Western market economy would be subverted, and America would wind up with a large state enterprise sector—foreign-owned.

Our natural resources would be managed according to the interests of foreign governments and their state enterprises. The policies of Eurofer, the European Common Market's steel cartel, are designed to bind us to their needs. Eurofer has decided to rationalize the Community's production base, to close antiquated mills in the Lorraine and the Saar, and to encourage the construction of new modern mills in the 1980s. These plans will require better qualities of coking coal from the mines of CDF, Veba, BP, Salzgitter, and Italsider in the United States.[7] And as they build their mills close to seaports, we will compete with them for Brazilian iron ore. American power in the world steel industry will diminish as Europe uses coordinated government intervention to place its interests above ours.

Should the federal government actively coordinate an American position toward this nine-country cartel? What should our government do now that 44 percent of the world's raw steel output in 1974 was government-owned?[8] How should it react to Eurofer's decision to halt steel imports, to produce semi-finished steel jointly, and to sell steel at bargain prices in the United States? Does our willingness to discuss steel as a separate issue in the Geneva trade liberalization talks indicate a change in how we approach the problem? Ambassador William N. Walker, the chief negotiator at Geneva, noted the American steel industry's concern at competing against "public treasuries." He said,

"A very persuasive case can be made for the American government to play a more active role in steel."[9] This would be reciprocity in action.

Should the federal government actively coordinate an American position towards the OPEC oil monopoly?[10] Oil is not merely a commodity. It is also the dominant source of energy. When its price is raised, so are the prices of other forms of energy. OPEC forces us to pay more for Algerian LNG. OPEC has forced the Third World to borrow from us with no hopes of repayment. OPEC has increased the costs of energy on our capital stock, thereby reducing the value of our plant and equipment and forcing us to write down this technological capacity because its productivity is substantially reduced. Piling these costs on the capital-formation sector has reduced the profitability of the European steel industry and the companion automobile industry. Can the United States be far behind?

Removing the Blinders

If we are serious about sustaining the competitiveness of our mixed economy in the face of these nexus challenges, we need federal intervention. Our orderly marketing agreement between the federal government and the steel industry is an example: (1) ailing domestic steel firms receive federal loan guarantees; (2) faster tax write-offs of plant and equipment and changes in environmental regulations will be permitted; and (3) when prices of imported steel are under reference prices, the Treasury will immediately begin a dumping investigation leading to the imposition of mandatory countervailing duties.

Two important nexus relationships are missing from our first orderly marketing agreement. While Nippon Steel, British Steel, and Italy's Finsider are able to set up a network of steel warehouses and finishing plants and the Japanese steel firms are able to assign technicians and product specialists full-time to American customers, the federal government has not required the steel firms—in return for government subsidies—to become more aggressive exporters. Their marketing instincts have disappeared as they became increasingly more frustrated with their inability to break through the complex Japanese domestic distribution system. We need a reciprocity agreement over steel distribution with the Japanese to make the orderly marketing agreement work.

Also the federal government needs to require the steel firms to reinvest their capital into the steel industry. Now U.S. Steel and others are diversifying into petrochemicals, coal, and other minerals rather than in modernizing steel. Our orderly marketing agreement may save a few jobs for a while, but it will not do the job that the Japanese, French, and Brazilians demand of their government-supported, privately-owned firms.

Federal intervention must include focusing enterprise goals on the critical economic problems for the national economy. Rather than denigrating government's role, we should encourage it to be more rational, to develop a national economic plan, and to save the market economy from the prospect of dominance by foreign cartels and other vehicles for inhibiting free trade among Western nation-states. As Thornton Bradshaw, president of Atlantic Richfield said, the free enterprise system never existed in pure form, does not freely regulate itself in competitive markets, accepts wide-scale government intervention, is a unique mix of private and government sources, and now is in need of an overall national plan for oil.[11]

We may come to see state enterprises as President Roosevelt saw them when he recommended to Congress in 1933 the Tennessee Valley Authority, a "corporation clothed with the power of government but possessed of the flexibility and initiative of a private enterprise." Those we establish today will probably be in fields where the risks are great, since private firms may well hang back in an age of capital scarcity, high energy costs, and reduced value of most existing technology. It is not surprising that energy state enterprises are first of the new line of federal public corporations to be proposed, for as Bradshaw notes: "No individual company—or likely combination of companies—can finance the massive research programs needed to make the crucial breakthroughs in nuclear fusion or large-scale solar energy."[12]

As W. W. Friedmann points out in his comparative analysis of public corporations, these new federal enterprises "should not be judged predominantly by ideological preconceptions. In most cases public corporations have been established in response to practical needs and they have often been most successful in ideologically uncongenial surroundings."[13] And the public consequences of these proposed federal enterprises will be in keeping with the dual commercial and social goals of market-sector state enterprises.

We have seen that France and many other Western countries prefer the commercial corporate form rather than a government ministry for a state enterprise. Whether the government is the sole owner or a minority shareholder, the joint-stock company or limited-liability corporation has been chosen as the legal form of organization for nationalized firms, enterprises merged through rationalization, and new business entities set up by governments. The state enterprise "must have the essentials of legal personality: it must be capable of suing and being sued, of concluding contracts; it must be liable in torts, hold and dispose of property; and it must have a separate name and a separate administration. Its assets and liabilities must be kept distinct from those of the government in general, whether or not it legally forms part of it."[14] It must not claim sovereign immunity in host country courts even though its home government can and will sustain immunity where such a claim is permitted—for example, Great Britain.[15] It must have a broad range of management decision making, be able to commercialize production and marketing systems, and be profitable enough to obtain investment funds from public and private sources, foreign and domestic, without the guarantee of its home government.[16]

Friedmann concludes by saying "There is little doubt that any genuine freedom of management and initiative requires that the public corporations, at least those of a revenue-earning character should have permanent assets freely at their disposal and not be dependent on periodical political battles in parliament."[17] No country represented in this book, the United States included, denies the ultimate right of government intervention in the commercial affairs of state enterprises when commercial autonomy acts contrary to the nation-state's best interests. This is the continuing dilemma of state enterprise capitalism.

Two federal laws do severely restrict the commercial autonomy of all business entities set up by our national government (e.g., the wholly-owned government corporations, mixed-ownership government corporations, private profit-making firms, private nonprofit firms, industrial establishments, and instrumentalities of the United States owned and controlled by the federal government). The Ramspeck Act of 1940 makes their employees (unless exempted as TVA employees are) federal civil servants, at the initiative of the president, and hence protected in their jobs regardless of economic conditions facing the enterprise. In common law jurisdictions, such as Britain and Canada, the rule is that state enterprise employees are not civil servants of government. In France, the employees of the older state enterprises, such as the banks, are civil servants, but the employees of the newer state enterprises are not.

The Government Corporation Act of 1945 subjects federal corporations, e.g., the Export-Import Bank, Federal National Mortgage Association, Federal Home Loan Mortgage Corporation, and the Federal Home Loan Banks*, to government budgeting and auditing requirements. It treats them like standard government agencies. On the other hand, most European countries audit their state enterprises using commercial principles wherever applicable. Since American commercial state enterprises would not be free to follow both their own dictates and those of the market, they are potentially open to more government intervention than are the fifty-nine commercial state enterprises.

These two laws show the need for further study of the status of federally financed, owned, and managed commercial state enterprises. In his 1948 budget message, President Truman stated the criteria for using the corporation to carry out government initiatives. These enterprises must be "predominantly of a commercial character—those which are

* Although this corporation has passed into private ownership, it is still classified as a government corporation by law.

216

revenue-producing, are at least potentially self-sustaining, and involve a large number of business-type transactions with the public."[18] These are still appropriate criteria. For the last thirty years they have been largely ignored by the federal government and the Commonwealth of Puerto Rico —the one major American political entity which has used government-owned business firms as commercial partners of private corporations to promote its economic development. On the other hand, the cement and milling business of the two Dakotas do follow these criteria and are also profitable commercial enterprises.[19]

In 1962 COMSAT, a privately-owned public utility subject to government regulation, was established. It has spawned such government-sponsored "private" firms as the Corporation for Public Broadcasting and National Railroad Passenger Corporation (Amtrak). It is evident that no Truman-like criteria were used to set up these federal government enterprises. They are an amalgamation of wholly-owned government corporations and instrumentalities of the United States' government. Believers in a mixed economy with a significant domestic state enterprise share cannot draw strength from these events because they have spawned three major problems.

First, there is a constitutional problem when the President appoints directors to their boards. Article II, Section 2 of the Constitution gives the President the power to appoint "all officers of the United States" with the advice and consent of the Senate. Legislation does not give presidentially-appointed directors for COMSAT, Amtrak, and other federal corporations the status of officers of the United States. These directors and the corporations they serve are in a constitutional limbo.

Second, there is the fiduciary problem. Presidentially-appointed directors are also federal officers. For instance, the Secretary of the Department of Transportation is a director of Amtrak. This forces them to comingle their public and private duties and to face potential conflict of interest and other ethical questions.

Third, there is the District of Columbia problem. Amtrak and others are incorporated under the laws of the District, which permit the board to remove any director, to dissolve the corporation, and to distribute its assets. Yet these things cannot happen. Only the President can withdraw a director's commission. It is unlikely that the District of Columbia dissolution law will prevail over the federal law setting up the corporation.

The future of commercial state enterprises financed, owned and managed by the federal government has not been given serious discussion. The prospect for federal chartering of the largest international private firms may stimulate thinking through how a federal energy enterprise might be incorporated without some of the above difficulties. Surely all foreign state enterprises should submit their plans for incorporation to the same federal agency. It could review their direct investments with an eye to insuring reciprocity. It could also grant them a federal charter to do business in the United States under direct investment and joint-venture terms beneficial to us.

A federal policy on state enterprise capitalism will not be easy to initiate. It would take at least five years for Congress to enact it. During this time the total sales share of foreign state enterprise capitalism will continue to grow at a phenomenal rate. New state enterprises will enter the world and American economies as foreign governments recapitalize, reinvigorate, and rationalize their local firms to make them fully-competitive state multinational enterprises. They have gained the support of international private bankers. There has been enormous change in their commercial relations with the United States. It would be strange indeed for such change in international business to end, for change is the law of the market economy.

Conclusion: America in the New Age

THE AGE of state enterprise capitalism, though still young, is now growing fast in industrial Europe, Canada, and the Third World, with the advantage of sixty years of change in relationships of government and business. When this age began in Britain and France, government thought its best interests lay in key ownership of petroleum firms. This notion persisted after the Second World War, when governments became bankers, owners, and managers of business firms, struggled to organize their state enterprises, and gradually learned that state enterprises must be free to compete in the market sector.

Today, as the web of restrictions and subsidies is broken and single-supplier monopolies like Petrobrás are forced from the controlled sector of the economy, workable competition for sales growth and profits is strengthening industrial nation-states. And the organizational advantages of international business are opening apparently inexhaustible cross-investment opportunities for state enterprises.

French state enterprise capitalism has been especially successful internationally. A quick review of its development illustrates how a competitive nexus can mature.

In the 1920s, the French government set up CFP, found it French private-sector partners, gave it its first source of foreign crude, commissioned it to provide at least 25 percent of France's domestic oil needs, and ordered it to end Anglo-American dominance of the international petroleum market. Control over European marketing of Arabian crude was the keystone of business success. France saw to it that CFP had exploration agreements in Iraq and Algeria and pro- duction and marketing systems in Italy and Germany and later in Canada and the United States as well.

By the early 1960s, France saw the need for a second French petroleum state enterprise to meet another 25 per- cent of France's domestic oil needs and help challenge the dominance of the "Seven Sisters." CFP, while not admitted to the "Seven Sisters," had been coopted by the seven major oil firms through agreements to share exploration zones and markets. This state enterprise could hesitate to do the French government's bidding. When the French state was weak, the government had to turn to its second petroleum state enterprise to explore in a friendly former colony or set up a new retail marketing system. Throughout the 1960s CFP and Elf-Aquitaine formed what the Com- mon Market called a domestic petroleum marketing system which monopolized the sale of petroleum at home. Over- seas, they competed against one another as if they had two different sets of shareholders rather than the French government as their parent body. In those days, Elf tried to follow government dictates, while CFP tried to slip away whenever it could.

The 1973 oil crisis brought CFP smartly back into line. Its main source of crude was cut off, and only direct French government negotiations with the Arab nations could re-open the flow of oil to France. So obvious was CFP's dependence upon its home government for power, prestige, and influence that little talk is heard now of its breaking away. By 1976, most of the traditional government-business relationships resumed, and CFP must compete with Elf for influence over France's petroleum policy and with CDF-Chimie, EMC, and others over France's chemical policy.

The new age of state enterprise capitalism developed quickly when government monopolies became market enterprises. After the Second World War, the nations of Europe and North America had to decide whether to continue controlling major industries. The development of new subsidy agreements in the 1950s seemed to give state enterprise capitalism a "socialist" life. We have seen, though, how subsidies retard economic advancement.

When state enterprises sought managerial freedom in the 1950s, governments answered with more restrictions and more controls. Europe needed new organizational structures, new combinations of resources and capital, and new cadres of professional management. With few exceptions it could muster only old habits of thought, and the number of deficit-ridden firms grew steadily. By the close of the decade, European state enterprises were strangling in a web of protection, subsidies, and market arrangements.

Ten years later, profound changes occurred. Under the compulsion of American foreign direct investment, the development of European Economic Community law against monopolies, and the resurgence of economic nationalism, state enterprises were set free in the 1960s to test themselves in the market. Pointing to BP and CFP as examples to follow, governments forced state enterprises to compete.

In half a century we have seen how single-supplier monopolies, state-subsidized enterprises, and other forms of government business entities became competitive and were caught up in the export trade and foreign direct investments. We have seen, too, how they became multinational business empires through which small numbers of managers control important sectors of the national and international economy.

Alternatives for the Future

A few years ago, when American firms dominated international business, we did not need to think about new ideas of economic organization and how to deal with their policy consequences. Because of the importance of government policy, any importation of state enterprise capitalism calls for an understanding of what national governments should and should not do when taking over the supply management of industrial goods. For example, just as the Department of Defense did when it sold the F-16, the proposed energy firm should sell its output above production and marketing costs. This involves competing in the market economy and making certain that the energy enterprise is a commercial state enterprise.

We are just beginning to realize that government owner-

AMERICAN DECISIONS

ship of business firms is of itself no panacea. The combination of private and state enterprises in the market economy is beneficial to the nation-state when employment, industrial investment, and market sector output are increased, when goods and services are sold above costs, and when domestic and foreign investors are willing to make loans based upon future expected profits.

But the opposite can also happen. The British government tinkered with its economy through demand management, devaluation, and wage restraints until it undermined the basic structure of the market economy. Britain now suffers with a declining industrial base, fewer people gainfully employed, and less marketable output. The sharp decline in industrial investment has meant insufficient factories and structural unemployment. Britain will slide from its status as a developed nation as its industry comes to resemble those in the Mediterranean countries of Europe.

Not everyone will be happy with this analysis: some would blame British state enterprises for underwriting the 25 percent drop in net industrial investment since 1965. But the real fault is government's insistence on industrial production—like the Concorde—whose sales cannot recover production and marketing expenses. Whether made by private firms or state enterprises, goods must be marketable. Nothing is gained by dividing the market economy into private and public sectors, as most American economists do, when the real dividing line for economic performance is the controlled sector versus the market economy.[1]

While Britain is experiencing deindustrialization, France, Sweden, and other European nations have encouraged their state enterprises to make investments which create industrial jobs. Since they also provide adequate resources from their market economies for new capital investment and for nonmarket expenditures (defense, welfare, and international assistance), their brand of state enterprise capitalism can succeed.

Americans must also wonder where Third World and socialist state enterprise capitalism will lead. Undoubtedly, the socialist nations are selling their exports and their maritime transport services—invisible exports—in competition against privately-owned American and government-owned European services. We cannot be certain that these nations and their enterprises are not dumping their services in Western markets, or taking from industrial investments to subsidize foreign economic thrusts. But when they seek Western loans without government guarantee, we can insist that they open their books to private lenders.

Whether or not socialist state enterprises are given opportunities in Western markets, there is no doubt that when governments insist that their state enterprises compete in the market economy, they can and will become formidable competitors for American firms. Since European state enterprise capitalism is being built in the United States on a "free enterprise" foundation, home governments must do as much as possible to build a strong base. The nexus seeks all the benefits it can from the American economy. When BP's Alaskan oil comes on-stream, it can be sold here at the upper-tier price under the American pricing system for new oil, whereas, "old" oil, which the United States majors control, must sell for some 60 percent less. Is this proper? Should the substantial profit go to reducing BP's North Sea debt, given Britain's generous 175 percent capital cost allowance? Should it be available to the British government for it to sink in its other state enterprises, particularly when British policy has forced them to reduce industrial investment, employment, and marketable output?

The future for foreign state enterprise capitalism in America will always be problematic if foreigners expect the flow of resources and dividends to go to their home governments. What is good for market-sector state enterprises and their home governments may not be equally good for the United States. State enterprise capitalism is worth pursuing only as long as American economic interests also benefit.

Whatever federal vehicle is established to finance, own, and manage American petroleum interests, it should be a commercial state enterprise with solid ties to the market economy. This will help establish a pattern of equitable commercial relationships between the United States as the host nation and home country-state enterprise nexuses.

Except for BP, the British state enterprise model is not for us. We must learn from Canada and the continental European nations. We must study how national governments and state enterprises (and other firms subsidized by governments) work together to create industrial output saleable in domestic and foreign markets. We should study rationalization schemes based upon well-thought-out national economic plans to create an energy state enterprise worthy of the market sector and a set of reciprocal relationships we are able to live with.

It is important today and for the future for us to attend to real problems of integrating a vibrant domestic state enterprise sector into the national economy. To do this, we must:

(1) Establish a procedure for determining whether a foreign state enterprise investor stands in good reciprocal status to the United States.

(2) Decide what type of federal or private firm should be the joint-venture partner for major direct investments in energy resources and minerals.

(3) Determine what should be the applicable legal framework for setting up foreign state enterprises and their domestic counterparts.

(4) Prepare appropriate administrative regulations that make the federal government-business firm nexus a more effective means for competing against foreign nexuses.

The intervention of the federal government in forming a national energy policy may be the single most important element in strengthening industrial state enterprise capitalism in the United States. Complex problems of investment need collaboration between government and business to provide the nation with the economic results it wants.

The existing haphazard federal government relationships to private and public enterprises cannot now manage supply, insure that American resources are not squandered in the cartelized world of European state steel producers, insure that American resources do not become the property of the world's governments, and rationalize American energy producers to develop a fair and sound nationwide energy plan for the 1980s. There is no national economic plan, no government-enterprise nexus, no set of commercial state enterprises to rely upon when the "world's product" is divided up. In times of scarcity, there is no mechanism for bidding resources away from other uses except through price auctions. The conversion of coal to oil and gas would become economical, by some rule-of-thumb estimates, if OPEC oil cost $15 to $16 a barrel, thereby increasing the cost per unit of heat by two and half or three times.[2] This price auction simply lowers the productivity of all existing capital stock even further. It requires the fragile American nexus to find the capital resources to invest in new technology as soon as the right combination of government initiative and enterprise management can be joined.

America in the New Age

State enterprise foreign direct investments have produced an unprecedented dilemma for the United States. Given the trend of foreign economic policy, the federal government, instead of regulating privately-owned firms, would have to join them in a domestic version of the nexus to protect American interests. The expansion of foreign economic power in America constituted the underlying $1 billion issue—the first sighting of the economic iceberg. These investments revealed the existence of a much larger presence and the dual economic and political challenges it posted.

In giving state enterprises freedom to investment here, Americans assumed that these businesses were similar to private firms. They did not see the nationalistic thrust implicit in this buildup of market share in the United States which, when large enough, would be used to reduce the market position of American firms overseas.

America has had direct investments by foreign state enterprises since 1966, but the state enterprise challenge that brought the CFP takeover of Leonard Refineries was trivial compared to the loss of Texasgulf to the Canada Development Corporation. There were indeed, good neighbor offenses, too—Polysar's rubber-mixing acquisitions for the purpose of eroding American market position in Canada, for example; or the United States-Netherlands-Canada tax treaties' ploy; or the monopolization of oil in the Northwest Territories and potash in Saskatchewan; or the takeover of American petroleum subsidiaries in Alberta. But these, like the coal investments of Veba and CDF in West Virginia, were questions that a foreign state enterprise might contend—until the federal government passed a foreign investment review code—were within the range of managerial discretion. The Texasgulf court case has discredited judicial review as a means for deciding whether a particular direct investments by a foreign state enterprise was appropriate for the American economy.

What is unique in the history of international business is the commitment by state enterprises to build up worldwide market position at the expense of privately-owned multinationals. Even before their first direct investments in the United States were initiated, it became evident that European governments were turning away from single-supplier monopolies and were turning them into commercial state enterprises within the Common Market.

The state enterprises consistently denied they were able to perform the miracles of regional economic development and industrialization. Had they been able to close the income gap between Italy's north and its depressed Mezzogiorno, the socialist formula for putting the government in all industries would have found favor in Brazil, Nigeria, Iran, and Malaysia. Had they been able to create world-scale, capital-intensive industrial jobs for all who wanted work, they would have been the panacea the Third World was looking for. They did have the loyal support of their national governments for transforming backward regions into developed nations.

The world market has decided the case. They are commercial enterprises worthy of financial backing and joint-venture partnerships. What is clearly beyond dispute is the commitment governments have made to the commercial autonomy of their state enterprises. These Western governments have set the example and picked those state enterprises to set apart as commercial businesses. What standards did they use? The Nora report made the case for France in 1968 that government subsidies must be withdrawn, state enterprises had to have the freedom to close facilities and lay off workers, and they must look overseas for resources, markets, and profits. In Brazil the government supported Petrobrás' desire to explore for oil overseas through production-sharing agreements and other joint business strategies. And Great Britain has decided to force its state enterprises out of the controlled sector and back into the market economy by following rationalization policies first suggested by the French.

These Western governments, in short, created state enterprise capitalism, the nexus relationships between government and enterprise, the fifty-nine commercial state enterprises, and their economic penetration into the United States. This was not what we had known before. Wall Street bankers, Madison Avenue advertising agents, and Washington lawyers were falling over themselves to serve these foreign investors.

The penetration of state enterprise capitalism into the heartland of free enterprise requires federal government intervention. Here is the dilemma in all its nakedness. If we do nothing, foreign state enterprise capitalism is bound to grow and prosper at the expense of free enterprise. If we permit intervention by the federal government, then we are initiating our own domestic variety of state enterprise capitalism. The most convincing solution as we approach the "age of state enterprise capitalism" in the 1980s lies in making the federal government a regulating partner in all direct investments by foreign state enterprises in the energy and mineral industries.

The problems of fitting state enterprise capitalism into the American political system centers on determining the proper role for government to play in managing multibillion dollar corporations. Nexus relationships are the most useful in distributing power between the home government and state enterprises and insuring the commercial autonomy of state enterprises. These are, of course, the instruments used by foreign governments to resolve their domestic economic problems.

But foreign governments are concerned with more than the internal relations of the nexus. Their larger design is to establish a new balance of economic power in the world. By their inability to act nation-states had become weak participants in the world economy vis-a-vis the privately-owned multinational firm. The restoration of national political power required the systematic recovery by governments of commercial prerogatives appropriated by private multinationals. Local nationalization laws were, in their view, a confused and sloppy application of this strategy; Canadians, French, and others had little use for them. Their own approach was to create commercial state enterprises.

A leading item on their agenda was to make state enterprises multinational. The question was how. As we have seen, in the 1960s, while insisting on sufficient investment at home, the Dutch and the Italians acknowledged an enterprise's right to license its technology, provide turnkey

231

services, go into joint ventures, and make direct investments, all overseas.

Spain and Third World governments, with their extravagant theory of government intervention covering everything related to commercial practice, delayed the coming of state enterprise capitalism. Their state enterprises remained single-supplier monopolies long after the political reason for this economic artifact had been forgotten. Competition at home was forbidden or circumscribed and these enterprises could not invest overseas. But the trend of the 1970s is plainly to favor commercial state enterprises in Spain, Brazil, Nigeria, Iran, Malaysia, and elsewhere.

Still, the willingness of governments to assert control, through orderly marketing agreements for example, is much in evidence. But now the fifty-nine commercial state enterprises are in no mood to agree to any restrictions that would drag them back into the controlled sector. There has to be a compelling national reason that coincides with an equally compelling commercial reason before government and enterprise hold a unanimous view on what is the problem and how it should be resolved. The 1973 OPEC crisis drew the petroleum enterprises closer to their governments and the 1976 overcapacity crisis in steel is drawing the steel enterprises closer to their home governments.

Foreign direct investment in the United States revealed that both government and enterprise wanted access to America's resources and markets. Only professional management could establish a fully-competitive manufacturing subsidiary in our market. A decision to invade the continental United States thus produced a corporate answer that would itself do away with what had been a traditional notion of public enterprise. For sixty years the government-owned entity had been thought of as inefficient, ineffective, nonproductive, and hence noncompetitive. Now extraordinary growth in sales and asset position plus continued profitability produced a new center of international business power, the state multinational enterprise. Would these be free of their home governments? Would BP, CFP, and the others place their own commercial success over the well-being of the nation? In the area of enterprise freedom, the state multinational enterprises remained committed to supporting the economic prosperity and political independence of their home countries.

Now for the first time Americans have to think hard about how they are going to combat this challenge. One alternative is the passage of a foreign investment review code, which has precedents in the developed world. If we really mean to proscribe direct investments by state enterprises, let us pass a law as restrictive as the Canadian Foreign Investment Review Act. But unless we simply want to be passive, this is not enough.

Active federal intervention means establishing commercial state enterprises to achieve national economic purposes. The genius of commercial state enterprises lies in their abilty to do their government's bidding without losing commercial autonomy. In entering joint ventures, America could protect resources for future domestic use without causing a diplomatic fury. The trick is to preserve the market economy, yet add a healthy form of state enterprise capitalism.

The commercial state enterprise is better equipped than government to recognize market opportunities and commercial advantages. When production sharing is imposed, the petroleum state enterprises rejoice, for they get their oil without incurring the great risks of exploration and discovery. The issue is not whether they had made the initial investment, but whether their government wanted them to share in the flow of oil as a consequence of domestic policy. But in the United States, no such compulsion for sharing exists, as BP, Veba, and CDF have shown. While federally chartered commercial state enterprises could be set up as partners for these foreign investors, there is no point in using them casually. All this argues for is a public debate on whether American state enterprises would serve the national interest.

There are two obvious ways to determine the facts. If the foreign state enterprise is seeking to acquire a domestic industrial corporation, then the Department of Justice along with its antitrust inquiry could be authorized to review the acquisition for its probable impact upon the control and management of American energy resources and other minerals. The Department could instruct the foreign state enterprise investor to find an American partner for those investments that should not be under the complete control of a foreign nexus.

The other road is through a foreign investment review agency under the Department of Commerce. If the agency establishes probable loss of American control from a foreign state enterprise investment, the American government could induce rationalization, bringing together foreign and domestic, private and state capital, resources, and managerial talent.

Possibly we will drift into the 1980s without a plan for competing in "the Age of State Enterprise Capitalism." The issue is more than whether we want to deal with state enterprise capitalism, the home government-state enterprise nexus, and direct investments by state enterprises. It is how we wish to make them serve our needs. In a time of the decay of the traditional political economy, a strong state enterprise capitalism grafted to our market economy is both a greater necessity than ever before and a greater risk. The nation now requires federal government intervention in certain domestic and foreign economic problems to help American business ward off and avoid serious dangers in the coming decade.

NOTES

Introduction

1. The evolution of state enterprise capitalism is described in the back issues of the *Economist, Financial Times, Entreprise* (now *Le Nouvel Economiste*), *Far Eastern Economic Review, Successo, Visión,* and *The Wall Street Journal.* European thought on the subject is developed in the *Annals of Public and Co-operative Economy,* published in Liège, Belgium. Additional information is cited in *The Management of Public Enterprise: A Bibliography,* authored by Nelson R. Maurice and Richard U. Miller and published by the Center for International Business Research at the University of Wisconsin.

2. "The Fortune Directory of the 500 Largest Industrial Corporations Outside the U.S.," *Fortune* (August 1977), pp. 226–235.

3. (Washington, D.C.: U.S. Department of Commerce, April 1976), vol. 7, Appendix K, pp. K–132, K–313.

Chapter 1

1. Statutes of Canada, 19–20 Elizabeth II, C. 49.

2. Texasgulf, Inc. v. Canada Development Corporation 366 F. Supp. 374 (S.D. Tex. 1973).

3. John E. Cooney and Tim Metz, "The Canadian Caper—Texasgulf," *The Wall Street Journal,* 30 August 1973, p. 8.

4. "Trudeau's Balancing Act: Economic Nationalism—With Continued U.S. Ties," *Business Week,* 30 November 1974, p. 6.

5. Robert Jamieson, "The Judge went all the way—against Texasgulf," *Financial Post* (Toronto), 15 September 1973, p. 1.

6. Texasgulf, Inc. v. Canada Development Corporation 366 F. Supp. 374 (S.D. Tex. 1973).

7. *The Wall Street Journal,* 8 October 1969, p. 4.

8. *The Wall Street Journal,* 7 October 1969, p. 32.

9. Status of Great Britain as a Reciprocal Country, 38 Op. Att'y Gen. 476, 482 (1936). Interview with Fred Ferguson, Office of the General Counsel, Department of the Interior, Washington, D.C., Dec. 29, 1975; cited in *Foreign Direct Investment in the United States,* pp. K–132, K–133.

10. Anthony Sampson, *The Seven Sisters* (New York: Bantam Books, 1976) pp. 62, 66.

Notes

11. "The Future of the British Car Industry," *Report of the Central Policy Review Staff of the British Government,* November 1975. Cited by Peter Bauer, "The 'English Sickness' Is Getting the Wrong Diagnosis," *Fortune,* September 1976, pp. 160–64.

12. Leonard Silk, "Market vs. State," *New York Times,* 19 February 1975, p. 51.

Chapter 2

1. Ray Vicker, "Iranian State Oil Firm Barges Into Ranks of Industry Leaders," *The Wall Street Journal,* 10 May 1977, pp. 1, 26.

2. *The Wall Street Journal,* 12 May 1977, p. 23.

3. "Tombstone ads," *Financial Times* (London), 19 May 1975, p. 21; 15 April 1976, p. 25; 26 August 1975, p. 6; 17 December 1976, p. 6.

4. "If Italy cannot borrow today, what happens to Britain tomorrow?," *Economist,* 20 April 1974, p. 104.

5. "Participation go away," *Economist,* 1 November 1975, p. 95; Roy Dafter, "In at the deep end for the new power in the North Sea," *Financial Times,* 14 January 1976, p. 16; Peter T. Kilborn, "The Sheik of Britain's Oil," *New York Times,* 29 February 1976, p. 7; "UK Agreement Widens Control of North Sea Oil," *The Wall Street Journal,* 17 March 1976, p. 4; Adrian Hamilton, "BNOC makes its presence felt," *Financial Times,* 7 December 1976, p. 21.

6. Roy Dafter, "Steel Policy and the oil boom," *Financial Times,* 11 March 1977, p. 2.

7. *The Wall Street Journal,* 2 August 1976, p. 14.

8. *The Wall Street Journal,* 31 March 1964, p. 6; 12 June 1974, p. 17; 15 January 1975, p. 17; 11 March 1975, p. 33; 20 November 1975, p. 39.

9. Christian Hoche, "Quand les Gascons revivent l'aventure de Montcalm!" *Entreprise,* 30 August 1969, pp. 31–33; *The Wall Street Journal,* 20 March 1970, p. 5; 21 May 1976, p. 3; 2 September 1977, p. 28.

10. "Tombstone ad," *The Wall Street Journal,* 20 July 1976, p. 27.

11. *The Wall Street Journal,* 10 March 1966, p. 13; 19 March 1970, p. 26.

12. *The Wall Street Journal,* 31 October 1969, p. 36; 24 December 1970, p. 10.

13. "Tombstone ad," *The Wall Street Journal,* 4 May 1976, p. 29.

14. Bylinsky, "The Japanese Spies in Silicon Valley."

15. *The Wall Street Journal,* 11 December 1974, p. 29; *Financial Times,* 6 November 1974, p. 22.

16. *The Wall Street Journal,* 5 September 1962, p. 30; 20 September 1965, p. 3; *Who Owns Whom (Continental Edition)* (London: O. W. Roskill & Co. (Reports) Ltd., 1972/1973) vol. I, p. Ge–134.

238

Notes

Part Two

1. Michael van Os, "State to raise holding in DSM," *Financial Times,* 23 November 1976, p. 24.
2. *Financial Times,* 28 May 1963, pp. 5, 17.
3. "The spectre of state monopoly," *Financial Times,* 10 January 1974, p. 22; "Knocking heads together," *Economist,* 3 August 1974, p. 62; Nicholas Colchester, "Veba rationalises oil interests," *Financial Times,* 16 March 1975, p. 24.

Chapter 3

1. Pierre Lindé, "Houillères: un atroce dilemme," *Entreprise,* 30 March 1968, pp. 32–37; "La morosité des Charbonnages de France," *Entreprise,* 28 July 1972, p. 35; Claude Rivière, "La difficile tache de Claude Cheysson," *Entreprise,* 13 February 1971, pp. 4–13; Robert Bacon and Walter Eltis, *Britain's Economic Problem: Two Few Producers* (London: The Macmillan Press, Ltd., 1976), passim.
2. "Bonn Pushes Denationalization," *Business Week,* 21 March 1959, p. 143.
3. Douglas F. Lamont, "Southern Italy," in Eric Baklanoff, ed., *Mediterranean Europe and the Common Market* (Tuscaloosa, Alabama: University of Alabama Press, 1976) passim.
4. C. Personnaz, *L'Evolution des structures dans un groupe d'entreprises publiques: les Charbonnages de France* (Paris: Mémorie de Doctorat, 1968); Beuscher, *L'Entreprise Minière et Chimique—Structures Internes et Comptables* (Paris: Mémorie de Doctorat, 1969).
5. "State-Owned DSM Provides a Lesson in Management Flexibility," *Business Europe,* 12 October 1973, p. 325.
6. *Rapport sur les entreprises publiques* (Paris: Ed. Doc. Française 4th trimester 1968, April 1967), p. 131.
7. Gabriel Aranda, "Affaires allemandes: Les dix premières present autant que les vingt-cinq premières françaises," *Entreprise,* 27 April 1968, pp. 78–89.
8. *Entreprise,* 13 January 1968, p. 9.
9. Rivière, "La difficile tache de Claude Cheysson."
10. Lindé, "Houilleres: un atroce dilemme."
11. Christian Hoche, "Où va la chimie française?" *Entreprise,* 14 June 1969, pp. 51–65; Nathalie Combien, "CDF Chimie: après le rétablissement," *Entreprise,* 27 July 1973, pp. 42–43; "Des chassés-croisés nécessaires," *Entreprise,* 25 October 1974, p. 69; Hélène Voillemot, "CdF-Chimie: l'oeil sur le Moyen-Orient," *Entreprise,* 1 November 1964, pp. 66–68.
12. *Entreprise,* 5 April 1974, p. 56; 27 September 1974, p. 47; "Any Offers Gentlemen?" *Forbes,* 1 April 1976, p. 21; *The Wall Street Journal,* 14 June 1976, p. 6; 16 June 1976, p. 23.
13. Michel Turin, "La nouvelle bataille du charbon," *Entreprise,*

Notes

13 December 1974, pp. 50–51; Jean Saint-Roch, "La ruineuse erreur du plan charbon," *Le Nouvel Economiste*, 12 April 1976, pp. 38–40.

14. "What's next," *Economist*, 22 June 1974, p. 62.

15. Roy Dafter, "Another major setback for British man-made fibre industry," *Financial Times*, 3 June 1974, p. 6.

16. "Pull up for a gallon of BNOC," *Economist*, 26 July 1975, "Survey," p. 18; Roy Dafter, "In at the deep end for the new power in the North Sea," *Financial Times*, 14 January 1976, p. 16.

17. Harold Bolter, "Steel: a compromise to please nobody," *Financial Times*, 5 February 1975, p. 17; "BSC to keep 13,500 jobs for extra two to four years," *Financial Times*, 5 February 1975, p. 32; "Investment questions for BSC in a weakening steel market," *Financial Times*, 9 January 1975, p. 14; "The steel works that is a 'politician's nightmare' ", *Financial Times*, 18 August 1975, p. 12; "Now for some steel sense," *Economist*, 2 August 1975, p. 77.

18. Bacon and Eltis, *Britain's Economic Problem: Too Few Producers*.

19. "The state and its monopolies," *Economist*, 27 November 1976, pp. 15–17.

20. Robert Ball, "The Grim Failure of Britain's Nationalized Industries," *Fortune*, December 1975, p. 98.

Chapter 4

1. Bacon and Eltis, *Britain's Economic Problem: Too Few Producers*.

2. Douglas Lamont, *Managing Foreign Investment in Southern Italy* (New York: Praeger Publishers, Inc., 1973) passim.

3. Istituto di Ricerca e Documentazione Luigi Einaudi (Turin, unpublished study), cited in "Italy's IRI: How Good a Formula?" *Economist*, 7 October 1967, p. 60.

4. Ibid.

5. Paul Betts, "Crisis point for Italian giant State companies," *Financial Times*, 4 March 1977, p. 4.

6. Stuart Holland, ed., *The State as Entrepreneur* (London: Weidenfeld & Nicolson, 1972), pp. 3–4.

7. Lamont, "Southern Italy."

8. Personal interviews with American executives in Italy.

9. Peter Seaborn Smith, *Oil and Politics in Modern Brazil* (Toronto: Macmillan of Canada, Ltd., 1976).

10. Werner Baer, Richard Newfarmer, and Thomas Trebat, "On State Capitalism in Brazil: Some New Issues and Questions," *Technical Papers Series* (Austin: Public Sector Studies Group, Institute of Latin American Studies, The University of Texas at Austin, 1976) p. 19.

11. "1975 Iron Ore Shipments of Companies," *Skillings Mining Review*, 3 July 1976.

12. Steven Rattner, "Abadan Refinery: Saga of Superlatives," *New York Times*, 8 June 1977, pp. 47, 51.

13. Rémi Sadoux, "C.F.P.: Le no. 1 française pour les benefices.

Pourquoi? Comment?" *Entreprise*, 18 October 1969, p. 16; "CFP may pull out of Italy," *Financial Times*, 27 August 1974, p. 31; Paul Betts, "Total-Italy plans to sell Mantua refinery," *Financial Times*, 23 February 1977, p. 58; "Arco's British unit is being sold to arm of French oil firm," *The Wall Street Journal*, 4 September 1974, p. 27.

14. William Dullforce, "Statsföretag opposes Government policy," *Financial Times*, 5 February 1976, p. 22; "Swedish steel crisis resignation," *Financial Times*, 2 March 1976, p. 20; Adrian Hamilton, "Problems of a state-owned conglomerate," *Financial Times*, 25 August 1976, p. 11; Fay Gjester, "Norwegian State oil go-ahead," *Financial Times*, 8 January 1976, p. 19.

Chapter 5

1. *Financial Times*, 30 December 1974, p. 16; 25 October 1976, p. 23; 22 October 1976, p. 31.

Chapter 6

1. "A Servant of the State," *Financial Times*, 23 April 1974, p. 21; Clyde H. Farnsworth, "The Eighth Oil 'Sister' Has French Accent," *New York Times*, 21 April 1974, pp. F 1–2.

2. Michel Drancourt, "Entreprise transnationales contre etatisme industriel," *Entreprise*, 22 March 1969, p. 139.

3. Rupert Cornwell, "CII future still uncertain," *Financial Times*, 29 January 1975, p. 32; "France unveils State plan for computer sector," *Financial Times*, 23 September 1976, p. 26.

4. "France: A Host of Troubles Plague the Oil Giants," *Business Week*, 3 February 1975, p. 30.

5. G. van Hecke, "Government Enterprises and National Monopolies Under the E.E.C. Treaty," *Common Market Law Review*, vol. 3 (March 1966): p. 457.

6. Craig R. Whitney, "West German Formula: Not Just Work, but Minimizing of Industrial Strife," *New York Times*, 29 September 1976, p. C 14; "West Germany II: Market forces, a web of influence," *Financial Times*, 18 October 1976, p. 12.

7. Jacques Baron, "Politique industrielle: la leçon de l'acier," *Le Nouvel Economiste*, 28 February 1977, pp. 42–43; David Curry, "French steel's economic and political stresses," *Financial Times*, 16 May 1977, p. 12.

8. "Les obstacles a l'industrialisation de la France," *Entreprise*, 5 June 1971, p. 151.

9. "Britain: a State Oil Company Takes a Private Loan," *Business Week*, 20 June 1977, p. 48.

10. "SEC Cautions Brokers on Trading Stock in Volkswagon," *The Wall Street Journal*, 13 April 1961, p. 26.

11. *The Wall Street Journal*, 17 May 1961, p. 20; "Denationalisation

Notes

of Volkswagen," *Economist*, 14 January 1961, p. 160.

12. "Ads in Dailies Helped Sell VW Stock to Germans," *Advertising Age*, 9 January 1961, p. 81.

Chapter 7

1. van Hecke, "Government Enterprises . . .," p. 454.
2. Ibid., pp. 455–456.
3. Ibid., pp. 456–457.
4. *Entreprise*, 30 March 1973, p. 79.
5. "Les contradictions d'une 'Gitane'," *Le Nouvel Economiste*, 4 October 1976, pp. 66–67.
6. "The British Thrust Abroad: Investments in Italy," *Business Europe*, 14 June 1974, p. 190; *The Wall Street Journal*, 10 July 1974, p. 10; "Les premières entreprises italiennes," *Entreprise*, 24 February 1968, pp. 55–59.
7. "Africa is a Second Home for Italian Oil Company," *New York Times*, 12 April 1970, p. 13.
8. "ENI's Fine Italian Hand," *Forbes*, 1 April 1975, pp. 38–40; *The Wall Street Journal*, 16 March 1976, p. 10; *The Wall Street Journal*, 7 July 1972, p. 19; *Business Asia*, 8 March 1974, p. 80; "Why Bechtel Won't Build Egypt's Pipeline," *Business Week*, 20 April 1974, p. 39.
9. "If Italy cannot borrow today what happens to Britain tomorrow?" *Economist*, 20 April 1974, p. 104.

Chapter 8

1. "State-Owned DSM Provides a Lesson in Management Flexibility," *Business Europe*, 12 October 1973, p. 325.
2. Jean Saint-Roch, "La ruineuse erreur . . .," p. 40; "Nouvelle offensive contre le charbon française," *Le Nouvel Economiste*, 20 December 1976, p. 33.
3. *Annual Report* 1973, Cie. Française des Pétroles, p. 20.
4. *Entreprise*, 3 March 1972, p. 92; 23 June 1972, p. 70; 1 June 1973, p. 65; 4 July 1974, p. 60; 8 November 1974, p. 87.
5. Hélène Voillemot, "Peintures papiers peints: mariages dans l'air," *Entreprise*, 9 May 1975, pp. 36–38.
6. *Entreprise*, 22 June 1973, p. 71; 20 July 1973, p. 31; Alain Jemain, "Castaigne dans le giron de la SNPA," *Entreprise*, 17 May 1974, p. 76; "Laboratoires Labaz, ou comment une filiale absorbe sa mère!" *Entreprise*, 5 April 1969, p. 49; Alain Jemain, "Dans les cosmetiques la fortune sourit a . . . Yves Rocher," *Entreprise*, 8 March 1971, p. 69; "Pharmacie: le sursis," *Entreprise*, 8 March 1974, pp. 52–69; Giles Merritt, "SNPA in new drugs takeover," *Financial Times*, 10 May 1974, p. 32; "Sanofi achète et va publier ses comptes," *Le Nouvel Economiste*, 2 January 1975, p. 88; "Sanofi rationalise," *Le Nouvel Economiste*, 20 October 1975, p. 97; Giles

Merritt, "SNPA acquires Roger et Gallet," *Financial Times*, 7 May 1975, p. 26.

7. Alain Jemain, "Pharmacie: les industriels preparent la seconde manche," *Le Nouvel Economiste*, 23 August 1976, pp. 27–28; "Elf-Aquitaine chez Pasteur," *Le Nouvel Economiste*, 11 October 1976, pp. 65–67.

8. Christopher Tugendhat, "An Unexpected Legacy From Signor Mattei," *Financial Times*, 19 October 1965, p. 14.

9. "Italie: Le 'boom' de la sidérurgie," *Entreprise*, 4 May 1968, pp. 48–56; Alvin Shuster, "Italian Steel Industry Is Paying Off After 30 Years," *New York Times*, 23 December 1976, p. 35.

10. Avison Wormald, "Growth Promotion: The Creation of a Modern Steel Industry," in Stuart Holland ed., *The State As Entrepreneur* (London: Weidenfeld and Nicolson, 1972), pp. 92–105.

11. Claude Rivière, "Montedison: 1ère affaire privée italienne; 6ème affaire chimique du monde; diversification et profit," *Entreprise*, 22 June 1968, pp. 36–47.

12. *The Wall Street Journal*, 28 April 1969, p. 17.

13. "More State Control Over Montedison," *Business Week*, 31 October 1970, pp. 28–29.

14. "Italy: Strong Medicine for Montedison," *Business Week*, 29 January 1972, p. 36; Anthony Robison, "Montedison: the plot thickens," *Financial Times*, 17 September 1974, p. 6; Hélène Voillemot, "L'affaire Montedison," *Entreprise*, 27 September 1974, pp. 34–35; *The Wall Street Journal*, 31 March 1975, p. 6; Paul Hofmann, "Montedison's Real Boss," *New York Times*, 27 April 1975, p. 7.

15. Jean Gloaguen, "Montedison: la liberté de gestion ou des pertes," *Le Nouvel Economiste*, 2 August 1976, pp. 18–19; "Controversial Montedison," *Economist*, 22 January 1977, pp. 70–71.

16. "Spain's Answer to the Multinationals," *Forbes*, 15 April 1972, pp. 58–63; *The Wall Street Journal*, 30 April 1973, p. 27.

17. Rémi Sadoux, "Volkswagen pilier nord de la GM Europeenne?" *Entreprise*, 10 May 1969, pp. 4–17.

18. *The Wall Street Journal*, 24 November 1964, p. 32; "Boost from the Bettle," *Economist*, 6 February 1965, p. 581.

19. "Volkswagen rubs it in," *Economist*, 13 December 1975, pp. 88–90.

20. Sue Branford, "New problems in Brazil," *Financial Times*, 10 September 1976, p. 24.

21. "Two Automotive Expansion Programs in LA Highlight Region's Strengths," *Business Latin America*, 25 December 1974, pp. 409–410.

22. Ibid.

23. "An awful lot of Beetles in Brazil," *Economist*, 13 December 1975, p. 89.

24. Alain Jemain, "Volkswagen: l'aventure de l'après coccinelle," *Le Nouvel Economiste*, 19 April 1976, pp. 56–63.

25. *The Wall Street Journal*, 13 February 1976, p. 10; "Sauve qui peut," *Financial Times*, 30 October 1974, p. 24.

26. "Why VW Must Build Autos in the U.S." *Business Week*, 16 February 1976, p. 46; Steven Rattner, "Volkswagen's Coming to Town,

but Which One?" *New York Times*, 28 May 1976, p. B 1; Charles B. Camp, "VW Picks New Stanton, Pa.," *The Wall Street Journal*, 1 June 1976, p. 4.

27. "Renault: Model for a Troubled European Auto Industry," *Business Week*, 1 September 1975, p. 38.

28. Ibid., p. 40; "Un nouveau Renault," *Le Nouvel Economiste*, 17 November 1975, pp. 65–73.

29. *Business Week*, 1 September 1975, p. 40.

30. "Renault en renfort," *Entreprise*, 11 October 1974, pp. 62–63; Giles Merritt, "Renault buys control of Clichy," *Financial Times*, 25 September 1974, p. 24; "Renault reorganises machine tools business," *Financial Times*, 29 January 1975, p. 32; Rupert Cornwell, "Renault machine tool deal," *Financial Times*, 23 December 1975, p. 13.

Chapter 9

1. Michel Turin, "British Steel: un colosse aux pieds d'argile," *Entreprise*, 27 October 1972, p. 81; Terry Robards, "British Steel's Long Road," *New York Times*, 19 May 1974, p. 3.

2. Robert Prinsky, "Hard-Pressed U.S. Steel Users May Get More Foreign Supplies Late This Year," *The Wall Street Journal*, 19 August 1974, p. 12.

3. *The Wall Street Journal*, 2 July 1976, p. 3; Roy Dafter, "In at the deep end for the new power in the North Sea," p. 16.

4. Peter T. Kilborn, "The Sheik of Britain's Oil," *New York Times*, 29 February 1976, p. 7; Adrian Hamilton, "BNOC makes its presence felt," *Financial Times*, 7 December 1976, p. 21.

5. "How Alaskan Oil is Reshaping Sohio," *Business Week*, 11 August 1975, p. 55.

6. "Malaysia approves London Tin deal," *Financial Times*, 20 May 1976, p. 24; Wong Sulong, "Pernas/London Tin: Final agreement reached," *Financial Times*, 1 June 1976, p. 18; *The Wall Street Journal*, 2 June 1976, p. 7.

7. Willard A. Hanna, "A Tale of Three Multinationals," *Field Staff Reports*, Southeast Asia Series, vol. 24 (May, 1976); Andrew Davenport, "Battle for Sime Darby," *Far Eastern Economic Review*, 3 December 1976, pp. 38–42; "Will anyone win the Darby?" *Economist*, 4 December 1976, p. 145.

8. Andrew Davenport, "Compromise at Sime Darby," *Far Eastern Economic Review*, 24 December 1974, p. 104; "Charting a future for Sime," *Far Eastern Economic Review*, 18 March 1977, pp. 103–104.

9. *The Wall Street Journal*, 18 June 1976, p. 26; 28 September 1976, p. 4.

10. Nicholas Colchester, "Veba rationalises oil interests," *Financial Times*, 16 March 1975, p. 24.

11. William Dullforce, "Lessons from the Swedish experience," *Financial Times*, 29 January 1975, p. 13; "Statsföretag opposes Government policy," *Financial Times*, 5 February 1976, p. 5.

12. "EGAM Points Up Woes of Italy's State Industries," *New York Times,* 9 February 1977, pp. 49, 58; Paul Betts, "EGAM to be dismantled by Italian government," *Financial Times,* 3 March 1977, p. 24.

13. "El acero en México," *Visión,* 15 December 1976, pp. 32–34.

14. Herbert E. Meyer, "This Communist Internationale Has A Capitalistic Accent," *Fortune,* February 1977, pp. 134–48.

15. "The New Sophistication in East-West Banking," *Business Week,* 7 March 1977, p. 40.

16. A. H. Hermann, "Going to law against a foreign government," *Financial Times,* 3 February 1977, p. 19.

17. "Jurisdictional Immunities of Foreign States," USCA Sec. 1602–1611.

Chapter 10

1. Albrecht Mulfinger, *Auf dem Weg zur gemeinsamen Mineralölpolitik* (Berlin: Duncker and Humboldt, 1972), p. 84.

2. "Oil: Governments Try to Bypass the Majors," *Business Week,* 7 December 1974, pp. 43–44.

3. *The Wall Street Journal,* 4 September 1975, p. 4.

4. "Canada to take up option on deHavilland Aircraft," *Financial Times,* 28 May 1974, p. 40; "Canada Gets Option to Buy Canadair Unit of General Dynamics," *The Wall Street Journal,* 17 January 1975, p. 19.

5. "Canada's Own Venture Capitalist," *Business Week,* 27 April 1974, p. 74.

6. "Canada Buys into Oil," *Business Week,* 24 November 1975, p. 36; *The Wall Street Journal,* 2 January 1976, p. 2.

7. "Sudan: Arab Loans," *Africa,* April 1975, p. 90; "Sweet Prospect for Sudan sugar," *New African,* January 1977, p. 41; John Waterbury, "The Sudan in Quest of a Surplus," *Field Staff Reports,* Northeast Africa Series, vol. 21, Parts I–III (August, 1976).

8. "Colombian energy: a stirring of nationalism," *Financial Times,* 17 April 1974, p. 21.

9. Hugh O'Shaugnessy, "Bolivia's mineral wealth, a gamble for the foreigner," *Financial Times,* 15 October 1974, p. 5.

10. Bowen Northrup, "Gas Up With NIOC?" *The Wall Street Journal,* 27 November 1973, pp. 1, 17; Guy de Jonquieres, "Shell in talks on Iran stake in U.S. chain," *Financial Times,* 28 November 1974, p. 1.

11. *The Wall Street Journal,* 5 November 1974, p. 6; 11 December 1974, p. 29.

12. "France-Algeria: Polemic," *Africa,* March 1976, p. 28.

13. "EIB loan for Ekofisk," *Financial Times,* 18 December 1974, p. 24; *The Wall Street Journal,* 2 January 1975, p. 23.

14. Adrian Hamilton, "Total may buy Arco outlets," *Financial Times,* 2 August 1974, p. 32; *The Wall Street Journal,* 4 September 1974, p. 27; 19 December 1974, p. 26; Terry Dodsworth, "Elf takes over VIP petrol stations," *Financial Times,* 7 April 1976, p. 10.

Notes

Chapter 11

1. Douglas F. Lamont and Huron Smith, "Economic Policy and International Corporate Strategy in a World of State Enterprise Capitalism," *Wisconsin Working Paper* (Madison: Graduate School of Business, University of Wisconsin-Madison, November 1976) p. 28; revised January 1978 by Douglas F. Lamont.
2. *The Wall Street Journal*, 17 June 1976, p. 19.
3. *The Wall Street Journal*, 24 September 1976, p. 2.
4. *The Wall Street Journal*, 10 March 1966, p. 13.
5. *The Wall Street Journal*, 19 March 1970, p. 26.
6. *The Wall Street Journal*, 21 May 1973, p. 19.
7. *Entreprise*, 5 April 1974, p. 56; 27 September 1974, p. 47; "Any Offers, Gentlemen?" *Forbes*, 1 April 1976, p. 21; *The Wall Street Journal*, 14 June 1976, p. 6; 16 June 1976, p. 23.
8. Michel Turin, "Les Charbonnages de France vont extraire leur charbon à l'étranger," *Le Nouvel Economiste*, 10 November 1975, pp. 89–92.
9. Ibid.
10. *The Wall Street Journal*, 8 November 1974, p. 6.
11. *The Wall Street Journal*, 8 October 1973, p. 12; 27 March 1974, p. 11.
12. *The Wall Street Journal*, 21 February 1975, p. 8.
13. *The Wall Street Journal*, 18 December 1975, p. 25.
14. *The Wall Street Journal*, 15 January 1975, p. 17.
15. "Big Money to Get the Oil Out," *Fortune*, December 1975, p. 20.
16. *The Wall Street Journal*, 7 November 1973, p. 31.
17. "The Tax-Treaty Ploy," *Business Week*, 17 February 1975, p. 54.
18. *The Wall Street Journal*, 2 January 1976, p. 2.
19. *Business Week*, 27 April 1974, p. 74.
20. "Controversial Montedison," *Economist*, 22 January 1977, pp. 70–71; Rhys David, "Montedison to use new plastics technology," *Financial Times*, 22 February 1977, p. 6.

Chapter 12

1. Terry P. Brown, "Shaky Showrooms," *The Wall Street Journal*, 26 March 1976, p. 1.
2. *Fortune*, December 1975, p. 20.
3. "Volkswagen would accept State holding in Mexico," *Financial Times*, 5 October 1976, p. 34.
4. *The Wall Street Journal*, 20 September 1965, p. 3.
5. *Financial Times*, 2 August 1974, p. 32; *The Wall Street Journal*, 4 September 1974, p. 27.
6. *The Wall Street Journal*, 19 December 1974, p. 26; *Financial Times*, 7 April 1976, p. 10.
7. Paul Ellman, "Elf to sell lubricants in Britain," *Financial Times*, 17 May 1974, p. 12.

8. DSM *Industrial Activities*, January 1976, pp. 4–5.
9. *Annual Report 1975*, Polysar; Interview with Clint Sykes of Polysar, 20 July 1976.
10. *The Wall Street Journal*, 5 September 1962, p. 30.
11. *The Wall Street Journal*, 5 September 1974, p. 10.
12. *The Wall Street Journal*, 20 May 1975, p. 24.
13. *Financial Times*, 8 June 1974, p. 11.
14. *The Wall Street Journal*, 20 November 1975, p. 39.
15. Ivor W. Boggias, "Saskatchewan Gov't Potash Takeover Eyed," *Journal of Commerce*, 16 November 1976, p. 5.

Chapter 13

1. "Why VW Must Build Autos in the U.S.," *Business Week*, 16 February 1976, p. 46.
2. Guy Hawtin, "VW of America sales plunge," *Financial Times*, 7 November 1975, p. 24.

Chapter 15

1. David A. Loehwing, "Arms Deal of the Century," *Barron's*, 20 January 1975, p. 3.
2. "Government Intervention," *Business Week*, 4 April 1977, pp. 42–95.
3. Eli Ginzberg, "The Pluralistic Economy of the U.S.," *Scientific American*, no. 235 (December 1976) p. 26.
4. Ibid., p. 27.
5. W. W. Rostow, "Caught by Kondratieff," *The Wall Street Journal*, 8 March 1977, p. 18.
6. Ibid.
7. "Davignon to Europe's steelmakers: slim down," *Economist*, 5 March 1977, p. 91; "The Steel Community Tries to Stabilize Itself," *Business Week*, 4 April 1977, p. 36.
8. Paul Lewis, "European Steel Industry Faces Worst Crisis in Memory," *New York Times*, 23 May 1977, pp. 41–42.
9. "The Outlook," *The Wall Street Journal*, 6 December 1976, p. 1.
10. Even such free enterprise writers as Irving Kristol and Leonard Silk argue for federal government intervention to protect the free market against the OPEC cartel. Irving Kristol, "The OPEC Connection," *The Wall Street Journal*, 22 February 1977, p. 18; Silk, "Market vs. State."
11. Thornton Bradshaw, "My Case for National Planning," *Fortune*, February 1977, p. 100.
12. Ibid., p. 104.
13. W. Friedmann, "A Comparative Analysis," in W. Friedmann, ed., *The Public Corporation: A Comparative Symposium* (London: Stevens & Sons, Ltd., 1954) p. 545.

Notes

14. Ibid., pp. 559–560.
15. USCA Sec. 1602–1611.
16. Douglas F. Lamont, "Joining forces with foreign state enterprises," *Harvard Business Review* 51 (July-August 1973) p. 68–79.
17. Friedmann, "A Comparative Analysis . . .," p. 568.
18. Harold Seidman, "Government-sponsored Enterprise in the United States," in Bruce Smith, ed., *The New Political Economy: The Public Use of the Private Sector* (London: Macmillan, 1975), p. 85.
19. "Living With Sin and Liking It," *Forbes*, 15 January 1975, pp. 38–39.

Conclusion

1. Bacon and Eltis, *Britain's Economic Problems: Too Few Producers.*
2. "Coal: still dethroned," *The Economist*, 20 March 1976, p. 77.

APPENDIX: GIANT INDUSTRIAL STATE ENTERPRISE METHODOLOGY (GINSEM©) FROM STATE DATA ENTERPRISE BANK©

All information in this book about state enterprises is extracted from the author's State Enterprise Data Bank. Tables A–1 through A–14 summarize the results of analyses made by the author using his Giant Industrial State Enterprise Methodology (GINSEM©) which is an analytical methodology for comparing the performance of state enterprises and private firms (by industry, country, and geographic region) and for comparing the performance of alternative sets of state enterprises (by industry, country, and geographic region) among themselves. The financial data on sales, net income, assets, equity, and number of employees (which is summarized and reported in these tables) for the fifty-nine state enterprises listed in Table 2–1 for the twenty-year period 1957–76 comes from "The Fortune Directory of the Largest Industrial Corporations Outside the United States."

Copyright © 1978 by Douglas F. Lamont.

TABLE A-1

State Enterprises, Their Combined Total Sales,
and the Percent of Their Number and Sales Share of
"The Fortune Directory of the 500 Largest Industrial
Corporations Outside the United States," 1957-76
(U.S. dollars in billions)

	Number of State Enterprises		Total Sales	
	#	%	$	%
FORTUNE 100				
1957	5	5.0	4.4	7.9
1958	7	7.0	4.5	8.7
1959	7	7.0	4.8	8.6
1960	6	6.0	5.2	8.3
1961	6	6.0	5.6	8.2
FORTUNE 200				
1962	19	9.5	12.4	12.7
1963	18	9.0	14.1	13.1
1964	20	10.0	15.9	13.1
1965	23	11.5	18.5	14.2
1966	20	10.0	19.1	13.4
1967	25	12.5	22.2	14.3
1968	24	12.0	24.8	14.3
1969	22	11.0	28.5	14.1
1970	21	10.5	32.6	13.8
FORTUNE 300				
1971	36	12.0	43.6	14.3
1972	34	11.3	51.1	14.1
1973	38	12.7	75.4	15.4
1974	41	13.7	134.5	20.0
FORTUNE 500				
1975	54	10.8	161.7	19.7
1976	59	11.8	185.4	20.7

Source: "The Fortune Directory of the 100 Largest Foreign Industrial Corporations," *Fortune*, August 1958, pp. 115-117; August 1959, pp. 123-125; August 1960, pp. 135-137; August 1961, pp. 129-131; August 1962, pp. 115-117. "The Fortune Directory of the 200 Largest Foreign Industrial Corporations," *Fortune*, August 1963, pp. 139-143; August 1964, pp. 151-155; August 1965, pp. 169-173; August 1966, pp. 147-151; September 15, 1967, pp. 140-144; September 15, 1968, pp. 130-134; August 15, 1969, pp. 106-110; August 1970, pp. 142-146; August 1971, pp. 150-154. "The Fortune Directory of the 300 Largest Industrial Corporations Outside the United States," *Fortune*, 1972, pp. 3-9; September 1973, pp. 204-209; August 1974, pp. 176-181; August 1975, pp. 155-161. "The Fortune Directory of the 500 Largest Industrial Corporations Outside the United States," *Fortune*, August 1976, pp. 231-241; 1977, pp. 1-11.

TABLE A-2

State Enterprises' Total Net Income and the Percent of Their
Income Share of "The Fortune Directory of the 500 Largest
Industrial Corporations Outside the United States," 1957-76
(U.S. dollars in billions)

	Total Net Income	
	$	%
FORTUNE 100		
1957	.2	9.4
1958	.3	14.2
1959	.3	11.0
1960	.3	10.0
1961	.3	9.0
FORTUNE 200		
1962	.4	10.4
1963	.4	8.8
1964	.4	9.4
1965	.6	11.1
1966	.5	9.7
1967	.4	7.2
1968	.6	8.8
1969	.8	10.4
1970	.8	10.5
FORTUNE 300		
1971	.5	6.9
1972	(.1)	(1.2)
1973	2.5	14.3
1974	16.7	51.2
FORTUNE 500		
1975	19.7	59.5
1976	19.9	52.8

Source: "The Fortune Directory of the 100 Largest Foreign Industrial
Corporations," *Fortune*, August 1958, pp. 115-117; August 1959, pp.
123-125; August 1960, pp. 135-137; August 1961, pp. 129-131;
August 1962, pp. 115-117. "The Fortune Directory of the 200
Largest Foreign Industrial Corporations," *Fortune*, August 1963, pp.
139-143; August 1964, pp. 151-155; August 1965, pp. 169-173; August
1966, pp. 147-151; September 15, 1967, pp. 140-144; September 15,
1968, pp. 130-134; August 15, 1969, pp. 106-110; August 1970, pp.
142-146; August 1971, pp. 150-154. "The Fortune Directory of the
300 Largest Industrial Corporations Outside the United States,"
Fortune, 1972, pp. 3-9; September 15, 1973, pp. 204-209; August 1974,
pp. 176-181; August 1975, pp. 155-161. "The Fortune Directory of
the 500 Largest Industrial Corporations Outside the United States,"
Fortune, August 1976, pp. 231-241; 1977, pp. 1-11.

TABLE A-3

Compound Annual Growth Rates of State
Enterprises for Three Industries: Petroleum,
Extractive, and Automotive, 1971-76
(in percent)

	Petroleum	Extractive	Automotive
Sales	29.6	17.4	16.3
Assets	16.3	16.3	11.3

Source: Douglas F. Lamont and Huron Smith, "Economic Policy and International Corporate Strategy in a World of State Enterprise Capitalism," *Wisconsin Working Paper* (Madison, Wisconsin: Graduate School of Business, University of Wisconsin-Madison, November 1976) pp. 26-27; revised January 1978 by Douglas F. Lamont.

TABLE A-4

Compound Annual Growth Rates 1957-76 and 1971-76
(in percent)

TABLE 4A

Compound Annual Growth Rates
1957-76

	Totals		Average Firm	
	All State Enterprises	All Private Enterprises	State Enterprise	Private Enterprise
Sales	21.8	14.9	7.0	6.0
Assets	25.4	16.0	10.2	7.0
Net Income	26.3	11.4	10.9	2.8
Employees	14.0	6.2	0.2	(2.1)
Number of Firms	13.9	8.4	–	–

TABLE 4B

Compound Annual Growth Rates
1971-76

	Totals			Average Firm		
	All State Enterprises	State Enterprises Without NIOC	All Private Enterprises	State Enterprise	State Enterprises Without NIOC	Private Enterprise
Sales	33.6	30.6	22.0	21.0	18.7	10.1
Assets	22.8	21.8	17.5	11.2	10.8	6.0
Net Income	105.2	37.7	19.1	85.9	25.2	7.5
Equity	16.5	14.3	13.2	5.5	3.9	2.1
Employees	8.5	8.1	3.5	(1.7)	1.7	(6.6)
Number of Firms	10.4	10.0	10.8	–	–	–

Notes: (1) Tables in Appendix show sales and net income and other totals by years. These form the basis of the calculations in the columns labeled Totals. Because "The Fortune Directory of the Largest Industrial Corporations Outside the U.S." increased the number of firms listed from 100 in 1957, to 200 in 1962, to 300 in 1971, and 500 in 1975, I have calculated the compound annual growth rate for the "average firm" to overcome this statistical problem. (2) NIOC (National Iranian Oil Co.) is excluded to show its phenomenal growth is not responsible for all state enterprise growth.

Source: Douglas F. Lamont and Huron Smith, "Economic Policy and International Corporate Strategy in a World of State Enterprise Capitalism," *Wisconsin Working Paper* (Madison, Wisconsin: Graduate School of Business, University of Wisconsin-Madison, November 1976) pp. 21, 24; revised January 1978 by Douglas F. Lamont.

TABLE A-5

State Multinational Enterprises

			1977 Fortune Directory Information			
	Rank	Sales ($000)	Assets ($000)	Net Income ($000)	Stockholders Equity ($000)	Employees
British Petroleum (BP)	3	19,103,330	14,925,935	324,615	4,862,138	78,000
Ente Nazionale Idrocarburi (ENI)	6	9,983,105*	12,803,525*	(37,026)*	1,561,125*	100,747*
Compagnie Française des Pétroles (CFP)	7	9,927,775	8,946,164	34,731	1,662,038	44,000
Renault	8	9,352,884	2,679,662†	(128,702)†	548,188†	241,259
Volkswagenwerk (VW)	13	8,513,304	6,144,450	396,173	1,611,331	183,238
Elf-Aquitaine (Elf)	20	7,536,225	9,770,720	340,108	2,410,557	34,000
Montedison	29	5,826,432	7,221,152	(195,019)	842,090	144,595
Dutch State Mines (DSM)	61	3,522,642	2,837,586	49,980	833,708	32,600

*Fortune estimate.

†Fortune August, 1976 data; 1977 data not available.

Source: "The Fortune Directory of the 500 Largest Industrial Corporations Outside the United States," Fortune (August, 1977) pp. 226-35.

TABLE A-6

Five-Year Growth Rates State Enterprise
as a Multiple of Private Firms 1971-76
(in percent)

	Petroleum Industry	Extractive Industry	Automotive Industry	All Firms in "500"	Average Firm in "500"
Sales	1.20	1.29	0.86	1.53	2.08
Assets	1.60	1.66	0.75	1.30	1.87
Net Income	1.17	(N.A.)	2.20	5.51	11.45
Equity	4.24	0.23	0.45	1.25	2.62
Employees	(N.A.)	1.32	0.57	2.43	3.88*

*Note: There was a decline in average employment for both state enterprises and private firms. The private firm rate of contraction was 3.88 times the state enterprise rate of contraction.

Source: Douglas F. Lamont and Huron Smith, "Economic Policy and International Corporate Strategy in a World of State Enterprise Capitalism," *Wisconsin Working Paper* (Madison, Wisconsin: Graduate School of Business, University of Wisconsin-Madison, November 1976) p. 28; revised January 1978 by Douglas F. Lamont.

TABLE A-7

Top 100 Firms Compound Annual Growth Rates, 1957-76
(in percent)

	State Enterprises	Private Firms	Average State Enterprise	Average Private Firm
Sales	20.3	11.3	11.3	12.5
Assets	23.2	12.2	14.0	13.3
Net Income	26.0	8.1	16.6	9.2
Employees	11.9	2.5	3.5	3.6
Number of Firms	8.1	(1.0)	—	—

Source: Douglas F. Lamont and Huron Smith, "Economic Policy and International Corporate Strategy in a World of State Enterprise Capitalism," *Wisconsin Working Paper* (Madison, Wisconsin: Graduate School of Business, University of Wisconsin-Madison, November 1976) p. 28; revised January 1978 by Douglas F. Lamont.

TABLE A-8

State Enterprises and Private Firms and the
Percent Their Number Share of "The Fortune Directory
of the 500 Largest Industrial Corporations Outside
the United States," 1957-76

	State Enterprises		Private Firms	
	#	%	#	%
FORTUNE 100				
1957	5	5.0	95	95.0
1958	7	7.0	93	93.0
1959	7	7.0	93	93.0
1960	6	6.0	94	94.0
1961	6	6.0	94	94.0
FORTUNE 200				
1962	19	9.5	181	90.5
1963	18	9.0	182	91.0
1964	20	10.0	180	90.0
1965	23	11.5	177	88.5
1966	20	10.0	180	90.0
1967	25	12.5	175	87.5
1968	24	12.0	176	88.0
1969	22	11.0	178	89.0
1970	21	10.5	179	89.5
FORTUNE 300				
1971	36	12.0	264	88.0
1972	34	11.3	266	88.7
1973	38	12.7	262	87.3
1974	41	13.7	259	86.3
FORTUNE 500				
1975	54	10.8	446	89.2
1976	59	11.8	441	88.2

Source: "The Fortune Directory of the 100 Largest Foreign Industrial
Corporations," *Fortune*, August 1958, pp. 115-117; August 1959, pp.
123-125; August 1960, pp. 135-137; August 1961, pp. 129-131;
August 1962, pp. 115-117. "The Fortune Directory of the 200
Largest Foreign Industrial Corporations," *Fortune*, August 1963, pp.
139-143; August 1964, pp. 151-155; August 1965, pp. 169-173; August
1966, pp. 147-151; September 15, 1967, pp. 140-144; September 15,
1968, pp. 130-134; August 15, 1969, pp. 106-110; August 1970, pp.
142-146; August 1971, pp. 150-154. "The Fortune Directory of the
300 Largest Industrial Corporations Outside the United States,"
Fortune, 1972, pp. 3-9; September 1973, pp. 204-209; August 1974,
pp. 176-181; August 1975, pp. 155-161. "The Fortune Directory of
the 500 Largest Industrial Corporations Outside the United States,"
Fortune, August 1976, pp. 231-241; 1977, pp. 1-11.

TABLE A-9

State Enterprises and Private Firms, Their Combined Total Sales, and the Percent Their Sales Share of "The Fortune Directory of the 500 Largest Industrial Corporations Outside the United States," 1957-76

(U.S. dollars in billions)

	State Enterprises		Private Firms	
	$	%	$	%
FORTUNE 100				
1957	4.4	7.9	50.8	92.1
1958	4.5	8.7	47.1	91.3
1959	4.8	8.6	50.4	91.4
1960	5.2	8.3	57.5	91.7
1961	5.6	8.2	62.3	91.8
FORTUNE 200				
1962	12.4	12.7	85.9	87.3
1963	14.1	13.1	94.1	86.9
1964	15.9	13.1	105.3	86.9
1965	18.5	14.2	112.3	85.8
1966	19.1	13.4	124.0	86.6
1967	22.2	14.3	132.8	85.7
1968	24.8	14.3	149.4	85.7
1969	28.5	14.1	174.0	85.9
1970	32.6	13.8	203.7	86.2
FORTUNE 300				
1971	43.6	14.3	262.2	85.7
1972	51.1	14.1	312.2	85.9
1973	75.4	15.4	414.7	84.6
1974	134.5	20.0	536.9	80.0
FORTUNE 500				
1975	161.7	19.7	660.5	80.3
1976	185.4	20.7	709.7	79.3

Source: "The Fortune Directory of the 100 Largest Foreign Industrial Corporations," *Fortune*, August 1958, pp. 115-117; August 1959, pp.· 123-125; August 1960, pp. 135-137; August 1961, pp. 129-131; August 1962, pp. 115-117. "The Fortune Directory of the 200 Largest Foreign Industrial Corporations," *Fortune*, August 1963, pp. 139-143; August 1964, pp. 151-155; August 1965, pp. 169-173; August 1966, pp. 147-151; September 15, 1967, pp. 140-144; September 15, 1968, pp. 130-134; August 15, 1969, pp. 106-110; August 1970, pp. 142-146; August 1971, pp. 150-154. "The Fortune Directory of the 300 Largest Industrial Corporations Outside the United States," *Fortune*, 1972, pp. 3-9; September 1973, pp. 204-209; August 1974, pp. 176-181; August 1975, pp. 155-161. "The Fortune Directory of the 500 Largest Industrial Corporations Outside the United States," *Fortune*, August 1976, pp. 231-241; 1977, pp. 1-11.

TABLE A-10

State Enterprises and Private Firms, Their Combined
Total Assets, and the Percent Their Assets Share of
"The Fortune Directory of the 500 Largest Industrial
Corporations Outside the United States," 1957-76
(U.S. dollars in billions)

	State Enterprises		Private Firms	
	$	%	$	%
FORTUNE 100				
1957	2.4	5.6	40.2	94.4
1958	3.5	7.4	43.6	92.6
1959	3.9	7.4	49.1	92.6
1960	4.4	7.4	55.7	92.6
1961	5.4	8.1	61.5	91.9
FORTUNE 200				
1962	15.5	15.1	87.4	84.9
1963	19.0	16.6	95.2	83.4
1964	23.7	18.0	107.7	82.0
1965	28.2	19.6	115.2	80.4
1966	29.3	18.4	129.7	81.6
1967	33.3	19.4	138.0	80.6
1968	35.4	18.0	161.4	82.0
1969	42.5	18.4	188.1	81.6
1970	44.0	16.8	217.4	83.2
FORTUNE 300				
1971	63.0	17.3	300.4	82.7
1972	70.9	17.0	347.3	83.0
1973	89.6	17.4	424.1	82.6
1974	134.2	21.2	498.2	78.8
FORTUNE 500				
1975	156.4	20.5	604.9	79.5
1976	175.8	20.7	671.8	79.3

Source: "The Fortune Directory of the 100 Largest Foreign Industrial Corporations," *Fortune*, August 1958, pp. 115-117; August 1959, pp. 123-125; August 1960, pp. 135-137; August 1961, pp. 129-131; August 1962, pp. 115-117. "The Fortune Directory of the 200 Largest Foreign Industrial Corporations," *Fortune*, August 1963, pp. 139-143; August 1964, pp. 151-155; August 1965, pp. 169-173; August 1966, pp. 147-151; September 15, 1967, pp. 140-144; September 15, 1968, pp. 130-134; August 15, 1969, pp. 106-110; August 1970, pp. 142-146; August 1971, pp. 150-154. "The Fortune Directory of the 300 Largest Industrial Corporations Outside the United States," *Fortune*, 1972, pp. 3-9; September 1973, pp. 204-209; August 1974, pp. 176-181; August 1975, pp. 155-161. "The Fortune Directory of the 500 Largest Industrial Corporations Outside the United States," *Fortune*, August 1976, pp. 231-241; 1977, pp. 1-11.

TABLE A-11

State Enterprises and Private Firms, Their Combined
Total Net Income, and the Percent of Their Net Income
Share of "The Fortune Directory of the 500 Largest
Industrial Corporations Outside the United States," 1957-76
(U.S. dollars in billions)

	State Enterprises		Private Firms	
	$	%	$	%
FORTUNE 100				
1957	.2	9.4	2.3	90.6
1958	.3	14.2	1.9	85.8
1959	.3	11.0	2.3	89.0
1960	.3	10.0	2.6	90.0
1961	.3	9.0	2.6	91.0
FORTUNE 200				
1962	.4	10.4	3.4	89.6
1963	.4	8.8	3.8	91.2
1964	.4	9.4	4.2	90.6
1965	.6	11.1	4.5	88.9
1966	.5	9.7	4.7	90.3
1967	.4	7.2	5.1	92.8
1968	.6	8.8	6.2	91.2
1969	.8	10.4	7.1	89.6
1970	.8	10.5	6.9	89.5
FORTUNE 300				
1971	.5	6.9	7.4	93.1
1972	(.1)	(1.2)	9.2	101.2
1973	2.5	14.3	14.8	85.7
1974	16.7	51.2	16.0	48.8
FORTUNE 500				
1975	19.7	59.5	13.4	40.5
1976	19.9	52.8	17.7	47.2

Source: "The Fortune Directory of the 100 Largest Foreign Industrial Corporations," *Fortune*, August 1958, pp. 115-117; August 1959, pp.· 123-125; August 1960, pp. 135-137; August 1961, pp. 129-131; August 1962, pp. 115-117. "The Fortune Directory of the 200 Largest Foreign Industrial Corporations," *Fortune*, August 1963, pp. 139-143; August 1964, pp. 151-155; August 1965, pp. 169-173; August 1966, pp. 147-151; September 15, 1967, pp. 140-144; September 15, 1968, pp. 130-134; August 15, 1969, pp. 106-110; August 1970, pp. 142-146; August 1971, pp. 150-154. "The Fortune Directory of the 300 Largest Industrial Corporations Outside the United States," *Fortune*, 1972, pp. 3-9; September 1973, pp. 204-209; August 1974, pp. 176-181; August 1975, pp. 155-161. "The Fortune Directory of the 500 Largest Industrial Corporations Outside the United States," *Fortune*, August 1976, pp. 231-241; 1977, pp. 1-11.

TABLE A-12

State Enterprises and Private Firms, Their Combined
Total Equity, and the Percent of Their Equity Share of
"The Fortune Directory of the 500 Largest Industrial
Corporations Outside the United States," 1966-76
(U.S. dollars in billions)

	State Enterprises		Private Firms	
	$	%	$	%
FORTUNE 200				
1966	12.4	18.4	54.8	81.6
1967	14.8	21.2	55.2	78.8
1968	16.7	21.0	62.9	79.0
1969	18.9	21.8	67.8	78.2
1970	19.0	20.6	73.2	79.4
FORTUNE 300				
1971	22.6	19.1	95.8	80.9
1972	23.2	18.2	104.1	81.8
1973	26.8	18.2	120.4	81.8
1974	34.2	19.9	137.5	80.1
FORTUNE 500				
1975	37.7	18.4	167.3	81.6
1976	48.5	21.4	177.7	78.6

Source: "The Fortune Directory of the 200 Largest Foreign Industrial Corporations," *Fortune* September 15, 1967, pp. 140-144; September 15, 1968, pp. 130-134; August 15, 1969, pp. 106-110; August 1970, pp. 142-146; August 1971, pp. 150-154. "The Fortune Directory of the 300 Largest Industrial Corporations Outside the United States," *Fortune*, 1972, pp. 3-9; September 1973, pp. 204-209; August 1974, pp. 176-181; August 1975, pp. 155-161. "The Fortune Directory of the 500 Largest Industrial Corporations Outside the United States," *Fortune*, August 1976, pp. 231-241; 1977, pp. 1-11.

TABLE A-13

State Enterprises and Private Firms, Their Combined Total
Employees, and the Percent Their Employees Share of
"The Fortune Directory of the 500 Largest Industrial
Corporations Outside the United States," 1957-76
(numbers in millions)

	State Enterprises		Private Firms	
	#	%	#	%
FORTUNE 100				
1957	.3	5.6	4.5	94.4
1958	.4	7.0	4.7	93.0
1959	.4	5.4	5.0	94.6
1960	.4	6.7	5.4	93.3
1961	.4	6.4	5.7	93.6
FORTUNE 200				
1962	1.3	14.7	7.6	85.3
1963	1.5	16.0	7.8	84.0
1964	1.6	16.1	8.2	83.9
1965	1.7	16.9	8.2	83.1
1966	1.5	15.4	8.4	84.6
1967	1.7	17.0	8.4	83.0
1968	1.8	16.3	9.1	83.7
1969	1.8	15.8	9.7	84.2
1970	1.9	15.3	10.3	84.7
FORTUNE 300				
1971	2.2	15.5	11.9	84.5
1972	2.2	15.8	11.8	84.2
1973	2.4	16.5	12.0	83.5
1974	2.7	17.9	12.4	82.1
FORTUNE 500				
1975	3.0	17.5	14.2	82.5
1976	3.3	18.8	14.1	81.2

Source: "The Fortune Directory of the 100 Largest Foreign Industrial Corporations," *Fortune*, August 1958, pp. 115-117; August 1959, pp. 123-125; August 1960, pp. 135-137; August 1961, pp. 129-131; August 1962, pp. 115-117. "The Fortune Directory of the 200 Largest Foreign Industrial Corporations," *Fortune*, August 1963, pp. 139-143; August 1964, pp. 151-155; August 1965, pp. 169-173; August 1966, pp. 147-151; September 15, 1967, pp. 140-144; September 15, 1968, pp. 130-134; August 15, 1969, pp. 106-110; August 1970, pp. 142-146; August 1971, pp. 150-154. "The Fortune Directory of the 300 Largest Industrial Corporations Outside the United States," *Fortune*, 1972, pp. 3-9; September 1973, pp. 204-209; August 1974, pp. 176-181; August 1975, pp. 155-161. "The Fortune Directory of the 500 Largest Industrial Corporations Outside the United States," *Fortune*, August 1976, pp. 231-241; 1977, pp. 1-11.

TABLE A-14

Compound Annual Growth Rates of State Enterprises and Private Firms for Three Industries: Petroleum, Extractive, and Automobiles, 1971-76

(in percent)

	Petroleum		Extractive		Automotive	
	State Enterprises	Private Firms	State Enterprises	Private Firms	State Enterprises	Private Firms
Sales	29.6	24.7	17.4	13.5	16.3	19.0
Assets	16.3	10.2	16.3	9.8	11.3	15.0
Net Income	23.6	20.1	N.A.†	14.1	58.3	26.5
Equity	8.9	2.1	2.5	10.7	6.9	15.3
Employees	2.1	(2.5)	2.5	1.9	1.7	3.0
Number of Firms*	–15–	–7–	–12–	–8–	–5–	–9–

Notes:

*Not a growth rate. Firms for industry analysis were selected only if data were available for both the initial year and the terminal year.

†Net income was positive in 1971 and negative in 1976.

Source: Douglas F. Lamont and Huron Smith, "Economic Policy and International Corporate Strategy in a World of State Enterprise Capitalism," *Wisconsin Working Paper* (Madison, Wisconsin: Graduate School of Business, University of Wisconsin-Madison, November 1976) pp. 26-27; revised January 1978 by Douglas F. Lamont.

INDEX

"Acts of God" clause, 9
Advertising, 178
Aerospatiale, 83
Agnelli family, 101–102
Agriculture, 119
Air frame industry, 138
Alaskan oil, 18, 38, 41, 142, 162–163, 225
Alberta, 146, 229
Alberta Energy Commission, 137
Alcan, 76, 103
Alcoa, 158
Algeria, 145–146, 212, 221
Altos Hornos, 130
Alumax, 143
Aluminum industry, 42; French, 6, 158; German, 55; growth rates for, 76; Italian, 101; private firms co-opted in, 128; reciprocity in, 41
Alusuisse, 101
AMAX, 110, 143, 158
Amazon region, 67, 69, 103
American Depository Receipts, 89
American Drill Brushing Co., 42, 172
American industry: Canadian policy toward, 10–11, 79, 228; economic policy and, 142–144; foreign investment and market dominance by, 28, 47, 158–159; fragmentation of European firms and, 98; French state enterprises and, 81, 109; German state enterprises and, 82; government support of, 63, 135–136; Italian steel industry and, 100; Japanese policy toward, 40–41; limitations on, 196; Polysar investment in, 87; reaction to foreign investment in, 8–9; state enterprises and competition from, 8, 9; state enterprise capitalism in, 4–5, 6, 45–46
American Motors Co. (AMC), 108
American Pecco Steel and Feralloy Corporation, 42
AMEX, 159
Amtrak, 46, 135, 204, 217, 218
Anglo-American Corporation, 120
Anglo-Persian Oil, 27
ANIC (Azienda Nazionale Chimica), 102

Antitrust laws, 178
Appalachian Resources Company, 156
Aquitaine, 74, 97–99
Aquitaine-Organico, 98
Aquitaine Total Organico, 98
Arco, 169
Argentina, 107, 121
Armco, 100
Ashland Oil, 139
Assets of foreign state enterprises, 37, 151–152
AT&T, 40
Atlantic Richfield, 18, 213
Austria, 11, 52, 89
Automobile industry, 37; forced mergers in, 74; French state enterprises in, 85; private enterprises in, 134; VW expansion and, 105–108
Avtoexport, 131

Balance of payments, 28, 36, 105, 114
Banff Oil Limited, 39
Bank of England, 120
Bank of Japan, 200
Banks, 88, 119, 159, 200
Bauer, Peter, 27
Bauxite industry, 71, 76
Beigie, Carl, 22
Belco Petroleum, 155
Belgium, 87, 92
Bogers, W.A.J., 189
Bolivia, 139
Bradshaw, Thornton, 213, 214
Brand loyalty, 180
Brazell, Reid, 154
Brazilian government, 52; exclusionary laws in, 44; intervention policy in, 67, 69–71, 118
Brazilian state enterprises, 4, 232; computer industry in, 198; economic factors and, 117; health care industry in, 161; joint ventures in, 103, 138; management of, 125; orderly marketing agreements in, 84; petroleum monopoly of, 33; potential multinational enterprises in, 31; private firms co-opted by, 128–129; steel industry in, 183, 211; VW expansion in, 89, 105, 186

263

Breda, 100

British Gas, 63

British government: British Petroleum (BP) policy of, 19, 27; British Steel subsidies of, 14; economic policies of, 224, 225–226; intervention policy of, 27; nationalization policies of, 26; North Sea petroleum policies of, 38, 44, 73; reciprocity and, 25; state monopolies and, 61–63; steel nationalization by, 55, 56–57

British Leyland, 27

British National Oil Corporation (BNOC): government policies toward, 61–62, 127; North Sea Oil policies and, 38, 73; private investment in, 88–89

British Petroleum (BP): Alaskan oil and, 38, 225; American economic policy and, 142; American investment by, 42, 155, 156, 208; distribution system of, 162–163; financial position of, 89, 159, 223; government policy toward, 27, 115–116, 127; management of, 123, 166, 173–174; marketing by, 181; North Sea oil policies and, 73; Sohio takeover by, 5, 8, 18–20, 24

British state enterprises, 4, 131; American investment by, 11, 41, 156; Common market and, 92; defect in, 205; domestic competition among, 28; French competition with, 98, 146, 169–170; government support of, 115–116, 117; orderly marketing agreements in, 83; shareholders in, 90

British Steel Corporation, 89; changes in ownership of, 56–57, 115; government subsidies to, 14, 63; growth of, 76; management of, 62; orderly marketing agreements with, 44, 213; North Sea petroleum policies and, 38

Cadres, les, 80–81, 81–82

Canada Development Corporation (CDC), 138; American investment by, 10–11, 42, 137, 208, 209; capitalization of, 160; management of, 185; Nederlands BV, 160; Polysar in, 86; tax treaties and, 160–161; Texasgulf takeover by, 5, 8, 20–23

Canadian Development Corporation (CDC) Oil & Gas Ltd., 138, 161

Canadian government: American ownership of domestic firms and, 10–11; CDC takeover of Texasgulf

and, 20–23; economic policy of, 26; foreign investment laws of, 44; government-business relations under, 52; intervention policy of, 118; reciprocity and, 25

Canadian state enterprises: American competition and, 8, 79, 158, 228; American investment by, 41, 47; cash reserves in, 85; domestic competition among, 28; joint venture with, 154; managerial freedom of, 86–87, 88; nexus partnership in, 137–138; petroleum industry and, 38, 39; reciprocity and, 10

Capital: British nationalized industries and, 63; commercial autonomy of state enterprises and, 126; competitiveness of state enterprises and, 72–74; foreign raising in domestic market, 9; government-supported privately-owned firms and, 33, 34; investment decisions on, 144; management of, 159–161; network of management contacts and, 177–178; OPEC countries and, 138; private investment and, 35–36, 88; regional income improvement and, 66–69

Capitalism, state development, see State enterprise capitalism

Caprolactam industry, 126, 130; in American markets, 9, 157; foreign state investment in, 42, 47, 61, 162; marketing strategies for, 171–172, 175–176

CDF, see Charbonnages de France (CDF)

CDF-Chimie, 97, 98, 222

Cefis, Eugenio, 100, 101

Celler-Kefauver Amendment, 18–19

Cepe, 138

CFP, see Cie. Française des Pétroles (CFP)

Champion Paper, 154

Channel Master Corporation, 42, 169

Charbonnages de France (CDF): coal industry and, 142, 229; establishment of, 75–76; financing of, 88; French policies toward, 73; growth of, 76, 97; management of, 76; state subsidies to, 58, 60

Charter Consolidated Ltd., 120

Chase Manhattan Bank, 88

Chemical Bank of New York, 89

Chemical industry, 6, 41, 96–97, 102

Chemische Werke Huls, 33

Chile, 121

Christian Democrats (Italy), 56

Chrysler Corporation, 27

Churchill, Winston, 27

Cie. Française des Pétroles (CFP):

Common Market and, 93; control over mineral resources by, 155–157, 158; diversification in, 98; establishment of, 11, 221; German-French competition and, 136–137; government policy toward, 56, 116; investments by, 42, 145–147, 154, 189; management of, 85, 86, 123, 169–170; orderly marketing agreements in, 80; stock in, 159; tax policies and, 81

Cie. international pour l'informatique, 81

Cigarette industry, 81, 92

Citibank, 88

Citrin Oil Company, 40

Clayton Act, 19, 38

CNA, 162

Coal industry: closure of mines in, 96, 97; dismantling of state monopolies in, 55, 56, 57; foreign state enterprise investment in, 8, 9, 11, 42, 46, 155–157, 229; French policy on, 142; German policy on, 55, 142; growth rates for, 76; reciprocity in, 25, 197; single-supplier monopolies for, 54; state subsidies for, 58, 61

Coastal State Gas Corporation, 158

Codelco Corporación Nacional del Cobre de Chile, 121

Colombia, 138

Columbia Nitrogen Corporation, 171

Comansider, 100

Commerce Department, 10, 46, 234

Commerzbank, 35

Common Market: French policies and, 73, 81, 92–93; investment decisions and, 144; Italy in, 93–94; Renault and, 108; steel industry orderly marketing agreements in, 14; VW expansion and, 106

Communism, 55, 64

Competition: Common Market and, 91–92; domestic, among state enterprises, 28; foreign investment in American firms and, 37; French state enterprises and, 76–77; government-business relationships and, 5–6, 53; growth of state enterprises and, 96; intervention and, 67–68, 194; investment of capital funds and, 72–74; joint ventures and, 169–170; orderly marketing agreements and, 44–45, 84; petroleum industry and, 139; setting up of state enterprises and, 8, 9; single-supplier monopolies and, 59; Third World countries and, 140; VW-Renault and, 107–108

Computadores Sistemas Brasileiros, 198

Computer industry, 143; French firms in, 81, 200; Japanese firms in, 40, 159, 201

COMSAT, 217

Concorde (airplane), 224

Congress, 8, 23, 24, 43

Connaught Medical Research Laboratories, 161

Conrail, 46, 135, 204

Conservative government (Great Britain), 63

Contracts, 9

Copper industry, 76

Corporation for Public Broadcasting, 217

Courts: foreign state enterprise limits and, 8, 229; socialist state enterprises before, 131–132; Texasgulf takeover in, 20, 21–23

Credit, 5, 36

Crown corporations, 51, 85, 86–87, 88

Cuba, 107

Customs duties, 92

Czechoslovakia, 55

DAL, 131

Dalmine, 100

Debt capital, 5, 6, 119

Defense Department, 202, 223

De Gaulle, Charles, 60

De Lilliac, René Granier, 189

Democratic socialism, 55

Denationalization of industries, 90

Denmark, 92, 161

Department of Commerce, 10, 46, 234

Department of Justice, 8, 18, 19, 234

Department of the Interior, 25

Department of Transportation, 218

Deutsche Bank, 35

Directed purchasing orders, 75

Distribution systems, 172–173

District of Columbia, 218

Diversification, 95, 97–99, 108

Divestment, 168–169

D'Ornano, Michel, 81, 98

Drake, Sir Eric, 115, 189

Drancourt, Michel, 80

Dresdner Bank, 35

Dubai, 139

Dumex, 161

Du Pont, 157

Dutch government: Common Market and, 92; dismantling of state monopolies by, 56; economic policy of, 51–52; European Coal and Steel Community funds and, 75; intervention policy of, 118

265

Dutch state enterprises, 59, 131; American investment by, 41, 43–44; government policy toward, 51–52; growth of, 96–97; joint ventures with, 103; management policies of, 60

Dutch State Mines (DSM), 130, 167; American industry and, 42, 47, 157–158, 189; British subsidies and, 61; commercial autonomy of, 123; corporate structure of, 171; European Coal and Steel Community funds and, 75, 83; government's relationship to, 51; growth of, 96–97; investment by, 41, 162; marketing strategies of, 175–176, 181

Eastern Europe, 107, 140, 162

Economic factors: foreign ownership of domestic enterprises and, 10–11; government support of state enterprises and, 116–117; management and, 185–190

Economic policies: compatible goals of business and government in, 114–116; intervention policies and, 126–127, investment policies in, 141–144; Italian state enterprises and, 94; joint-venture contracts and, 7; limits on foreign investment and, 25–29; management and, 168; need for, 227; state enterprises in U.S. and, 142–144

Ecopetrol, 139

Ecuador, 138

Electricity industry, 40–41, 55, 143

Electrônica Digital, 198

Elf-Aquitaine, 221–222; American industry and, 38–39, 40, 156, 158; Common Market and, 93; French policies toward, 73, 116; health care investments of, 180; investment decisionmaking in, 42, 145–147; management of, 85, 86, 123, 169, 185, 189; mergers in, 74; tax policies and, 81

Elf-Aquitaine U.S.A., Inc., 39

Elf-Erap Group, 38, 73

Elf Oil Exploration and Production, 39

EMC, see Enterprise Miniere et Chimique (EMC)

Energy industry, 6, 195

ENI: Common Market and, 93–94; credit problems of, 36; government policy toward, 56, 127; growth of, 99–102; management of, 123; regional income and, 68

Enso Gutzeit, 154

Ente Autonomo de Gestione per le Aziende Mineraire Metallurgiche (EGAM), 127

Enterprise (journal), 80

Enterprise Miniere et Chimique (EMC), 222; creation of, 58–59; French policies toward, 73; management of, 85; multinational corporations and, 76

Eurofer, 211–212

European Common Market, see Common Market

European Coal and Steel Community, 56, 75, 83

Executive branch: foreign control of American industry and, 18, 20, 23, 43; reciprocity and, 24–25

Export-Import Bank, 216

Export market: foreign state enterprises and, 12, 34, 104; Groupement d'intérêts économique for, 108–109; VW expansion and, 106, 107

Exxon, 8, 100

Fabian socialism, 52

Federal Home Loan Bank, 216

Federal Home Loan Mortgage Corporation, 216

Federal National Mortgage Association, 216

Federal Reserve System, 200, 202

Feltham, Ivan R., 21–22

Fertilizer industry, 42, 59

Fiat, 103, 105, 139

Financial Post (Toronto), 22

Financial Times (London), 24, 80

Finland, 84, 154

Finsider, 44, 100, 101, 213

First National Bank of Chicago, 131

Forced mergers, 72, 74

Ford Motor Company, 105

Foreign Direct Investment in the United States (Department of Commerce), 10, 25, 46

Foreign Investment Review Act (Canada), 25, 44, 209, 233

Fortune directories: comparative international from, 36; foreign state enterprises on, 4, 30; Italian firms on, 101; Japanese firms on, 41; labor force information from, 36; orderly marketing agreements and, 83, 84; sales listings in, 34–35; VW-Renault comparisons on, 107

French government: BP takeover of Sohio and, 24; business links to, 5, 51, 52; CFP established by, 11, 221; coal industry and, 142; debt capital loans from, 119; domestic communism and, 55; economic policy of,

IBM, 198
India, 76
Industrialization, 65, 69, 71
Industrial statism, 82
Inflation, 37, 63
Instituto Nacional de Industria, 52, 76, 103, 154
Internal Revenue Service, 176
Intervention: capital-intensive industrial development and, 69–72; competitiveness of state enterprises and, 72–74; European government views on, 26–27; forced mergers in, 72, 74; government-business relations and, 6; increase in use of, 118; national economic policy and, 213, 232; orderly marketing agreements and, 79–84; reciprocity and, 193, 194; regional income improvements through, 66–69; weakness of, 27
Intrafirm transfer pricing, 68, 71, 75
Investments: in American firms, 4–5, 8–9, 37, 41–43, 151–163, 179–180; British single-supplier monopolies and, 61–62; categories of, 42; competitiveness of state enterprises and, 72–74; government-business relations in, 5, 144–147; growth of state enterprises and, 95, 103–104, 224–225; guidelines for, 141–144; host country policies on, 28, 209–210; joint venture, *see* Joint venture investments; market dominance by American industries and, 158–159; nexus stability and, 176–177; private capital in, 88, 206–207; reciprocity in American policy and, 43–47; regional income improvements with, 66–69; resources for new market position through, 158; returns from, 159–163, 180–184; secure sources of raw materials from, 155–157; state enterprise capitalism and, 139–140; state monopolies and, 57; strong American market through, 157–158; Third World countries and, 121–122; VW expansion and, 105
Iran, 107, 139, 229, 232
Iraq, 221
Iraq Petroleum, 27
Ireland, 92
IRI, 27, 56, 68, 94, 100, 101
Iron industry: French policies on, 6; German control over, 55; growth rates for, 76; orderly marketing agreements in, 44; monopolies in, 54, 55, 56, 57
Iscor, 76, 83
Israel, 138

Italian government: domestic communism in, 55; economic policy of, 26; intervention policy of, 27; intrafirm transfer pricing of, 68, 71; regional income improvement by, 67–69, 229; state monopolies and, 56; subsidies from, 63
Italian state enterprises: Common Market and, 92, 93–94; credit problems of, 36; domestic competition among, 28; government support of, 117; growth of, 75; health care industry in, 161; investment in American resources by, 156; joint ventures with, 103; orderly marketing agreements in, 83; private sector and, 27; shareholders in, 90; socialist state enterprises with, 131
Italsider, 46, 76, 83, 100, 101
ITT, 81

Japan: American market dominance and, 159; bank laws in, 200; exclusionary laws in, 44; government-business links in, 5; high-technology electronics in, 40–41, 143, 198, 201; joint-venture contracts in, 6–7; labor force in steel industry of, 62; orderly marketing agreements in, 44–45, 84; privately-owned firms supported by, 33; state enterprise capitalism in, 119–120
Japan, Inc., 6
Java, 67
Jeep (automobile), 108
J.I. Case, 110
Joint-venture investments: Canadian, 154; commercial autonomy for management in, 123; competition and, 169–170; economic power from, 6–7; growth through, 102–103; private firms coopted in, 129; socialist state enterprises in, 131; Third World countries in, 140–141, 194; Vale do Rio Doce and, 30
Justice Department, 8, 18, 19, 234

Kobe Steel, 76
Kondratieff wave, 207, 208–209, 211
Krupp, 33, 139, 162
Kubitschek, 70
Kuhn Loeb & Co., 39
Kuwait, 139
Kymi Kymmene, 154

Labo Electrônica, 198
Labor force, 36–37
Labour government (Great Britain), 56, 57, 62, 63, 116
Laissez faire policy, 51–52, 90

Latex industry, 42
Latin America, 12, 94
Lead industry, 55
Leaseholdings, 9, 13, 43–44, 193
Laws: commercial autonomy of management under, 215–216; mergers of state enterprises under, 38–39; socialist state enterprises under, 131–132
Leiding, Rudolph, 187
Leonard Refineries, 39–40, 154, 159, 228
Libya, 139
L. M. Ericsson, 81
Lockheed, 135
London Multinational Bank, 35
London Tin Corporation, 120, 139
Lonhro, 139
Lotz, Kurt, 187
Luxembourg, 92

McLernon, James W., 165–166, 188
Malaysia, 120, 139, 229, 232
Management: Canadian crown corporations and, 86–87; capital supply and, 159–161; commercial autonomy in, 122–125; distribution system and, 172–173; economic policies of home government and, 168; economic power and, 185–190; entrepreneurial tasks in, 178; forced mergers and, 74; French *les cadres* in, 80–81; government-business relationship and, 9–10, 52, 60–61; intervention policies and, 72; leadership in, 165–167; network of contacts in, 177–178; organization structure in, 170–171; semiautonomous teams in, 173–174; state enterprise dependence on home government in, 84–86; state subsidies to enterprises and, 59; strategic corporate planning in, 133–134; Sweden's Statsföretag and, 87–88; Third World investments and, 121, 122; worker participation in, 26
M&T Chemicals, 39
Manufacturing sector, 119
Marché ordonné, 80
Martin Oil Services, 40, 154
Mattei, Enrico, 100
Mergers, 38–40, 72, 74
Metzeler, 98
Mexico, 35, 105–106, 121, 168
Mezzogiorno, Italy, 67, 68, 229
Microtechnology Corporation, 110
Mineral Leasing Act of 1920, 24
Mineral resources: foreign enterprise investment in American, 9, 46, 130;

French policy on, 75–77; reciprocity agreements for, 10, 12–13
Mines Domaniales de Potasse d'Alsace, 58
Minicomputers industry, 200–201
Mitsubishi, 162
Mitsui, 6–7, 110, 143, 158
Monopolies: failure of, 54–56; French policies on, 73; government policies on, 52, 229; intervention and, 66; Nora's attack on, 57–61; petroleum industry, 33, 92–93; Third World countries and, 121
Monsanto, 101
Montedison, 68, 90, 101, 102, 161–162
Morandat, Yvon, 60
Morgan Guaranty Bank, 88
Morflot American Shipping Inc. (Moram), 131
Motta desserts, 9
Multilateralism, 57

National Coal Board, 83, 89; establishment of, 56; growth rate for, 76; reciprocity and, 25, 157; subsidies for, 61, 63
National Iranian Oil Company, 33, 72, 138, 139
Nationalization, 26, 63, 121
NATO, 204
Natural gas industries, 38–40, 42
Netherlands, *see* Dutch government; Dutch state enterprises
New York Times, 80
Nexus: development of, 6; division of responsibility within, 117–118; need for reciprocity agreements with, 13; orderly marketing agreements and, 44–45; state enterprises as example of, 7
Nigeria, 229, 232
Nigerian Oil, 138
Nippon Steel, 76, 213
Nipro, Inc., 171, 175–176
Nora, Simon, 57–61
Nora Report, 75–76, 84, 230
Nordhoff, Heinz, 186
Norsk Hydro, 76, 170; capital support for, 35; government control over, 35, 90, 125, 168; joint ventures with, 103; North Sea oil and, 73, 168
North Sea petroleum: British policies on, 38, 61, 115–116, 127, 163, 175, 225; French policies on, 73, 146; joint ventures in, 103, 170; Norway in, 168; reciprocity in, 25, 44
Norwegian government: business relations with, 52; economic policy of, 26; intervention policy of, 118

Norwegian state enterprises: domestic competition among, 28; joint ventures with, 103; management of, 60, 125; North Sea oil and, 73, 146, 168; shareholders in, 90
Novamont, 161
Nuclear power industry, 81, 204, 207
Nypro, 175

Occidental Petroleum, 169
Office nationale industriel de l'azote, 58–59
Oil industries, see Petroleum and petrochemical industries
Oil Shale Corporation, 38
Old Ben Coal Company, 156
Omnimedic, 161
OPEC nations, 137; American position on, 212, 227; BP-Sohio takeover and, 163; challengers to, 138–139; international market position of, 33; management in, 72; results of, 121
Orderly marketing agreements, 203–209; competition and, 72, 84; French use of, 79–82, 92; German use of, 82–83, 137; intervention with, 79–84; meaning of term, 79–80; steel industry and, 14, 44–45, 212–213; subsidies replaced by, 83–84; VW expansion and, 106

Paint industry, 98
Pechiney Ugine Kuhlmann, 6–7, 110, 143
Pemex, 121
Penn Central, 45
Perkins, Stuart, 165
Pernas, 120–121
Petrobrás, 52, 69–71, 72, 125, 138, 139
Petro-Canada, 138
Petroleum and petrochemical industries: American policy and, 142–143; BP-Sohio takeover and, 18–20; Brazil's Petrobras in, 70; Canadian policy on, 138; challengers to OPEC in, 138–139; ENI's growth in, 99–102; European Economic Commission on, 92–93; foreign investment in American firms in, 6, 9, 11, 43–44, 46, 154; French-German rivalry in, 136–137; French state enterprises in, 61, 73, 81–82, 85, 92–93, 116, 169–170, 221–222; German state enterprises in, 55, 82; government-business relationships in, 52; government shares in, 90; growth rates for, 134; investment decisionmaking in, 41, 42, 145–147; legal restraints on, 8; mergers in, 38–40; reciproc-

ity in, 10, 12–13, 44, 196, 197; state monopolies in, 33, 56, 57; see also North Sea petroleum; OPEC nations
Petromin, 138
Petroven (Petróles Venezolanos), 138, 139
Peugeot, 37
Pharmaceutical industry, 138, 161
Phosphate industry, 8, 41, 42, 143, 197
Platte-Bonn-Mauser, 98
Poclain, 33, 110
Poland, 131
Polysar, Limited, 137; American investment by, 47, 189; Canadian policy and, 10–11, 158, 228; CDC-Texasgulf takeover and, 21; lack of Fortune listing for, 34; management of, 86–87; marketing strategy of, 171–172, 181; tax benefits to, 161
Polysar Latex, 21, 171
Potash industry, 92, 143; monopolies in, 54, 56, 229; subsidies to, 58–59
PPG, 101
Precision National Leasing Corporation, 172
Preussig, 89
Pricing policies, 54, 63
Private sector: autonomy of state enterprises and, 128; dominance of state enterprises over, 134; government relationships with, 5, 33–34; growth rates for, 79; management skills in, 9; risk capital from, 26, 35–36; state enterprises and, 6–7, 28, 88, 128–130
Production systems, 164–184
Profits, 113
Pruett & Hughes, 39, 158
Public land leases, 43–44
Puerto Rico, 217

Railroad state enterprises, 45, 46
Ramspeck Act, 216
Rationalization: autonomy of state enterprises and, 126; competition and, 72; diversification and, 97; economic policy under, 26; French policy toward, 6, 52, 73; goals of nexus and, 117; orderly marketing agreements and, 44; Renault in, 108
Reciprocity, 193–202; American market and, 10, 43–47; BP-Sohio takeover and, 38; CDC and, 23–25; foreign reaction to, 24; Japanese firms and, 41; magnitude of problem in, 197; mergers and, 38–40; National Coal Board and, 157; need